# SING
## TO THE LORD
### AN
# OLD
# SONG

MEDITATIONS ON
CLASSIC HYMNS

RICHARD H. SCHMIDT

Forward Movement

inspire disciples. empower evangelists.

# SING
## TO THE LORD
## AN OLD
# SONG

### MEDITATIONS ON
### CLASSIC HYMNS

RICHARD H. SCHMIDT

FORWARD MOVEMENT
CINCINNATI, OHIO

# BOOKS BY RICHARD H. SCHMIDT

*Sages, Saints & Seers: A Breviary of Spiritual Masters*
(Church Publishing, New York, 2015)

*A Gracious Rain: A Devotional Commentary on the Prayers
of the Church Year* (Church Publishing, New York, 2008)

*God Seekers: Twenty Centuries of Christian Spiritualities*
(Wm. H. Eerdmans, Grand Rapids, 2008)

*Life Lessons from Alpha to Omega* (Church Publishing,
New York, 2005)

*Praises, Prayers & Curses: Conversations with the Psalms*
(Forward Movement, Cincinnati, 2005)

*Glorious Companions: Five Centuries of Anglican
Spirituality* (Wm. H. Eerdmans, Grand Rapids, 2002)

# CONTENTS

# SING
## TO THE LORD
### AN
## OLD
# SONG

# PREFACE

Tears don't often come to my eyes in church, but when they do, it's usually because of a hymn—not a sermon, not a biblical or liturgical text, not the beauty of the architecture or a stained-glass window, but a song. I'd be happy with a worship service consisting almost entirely of singing. So important are hymns to me that when I sought a church as a young man, I chose the denomination that sang the hymns I liked.

Hymns are poems set to music. A good musical setting adds color to the poem, brings out nuances of meaning that might otherwise be overlooked, and helps cement the poem in the singer's memory. A compelling tune often initially attracts me to a hymn and draws the text to my attention. I have suggested a suitable tune (occasionally two tunes) for each text discussed in this book, and settings for most of the hymns I discuss in this book can be found in the appendix. Many of these tunes can be found in modern hymnals; all can be found at Hymnary.org.

In my private devotions, I often reflect on a hymn text and let it probe my mind and guide my praying. The meditations in this book are based on hymns I have come to love over the years. Because each hymn engenders a unique response, these meditations differ widely. Each begins with a few sentences on the authorship and history of the hymn. Then

comes an expository section with comments on each stanza.
The exposition may discuss the hymn's biblical background,
its theology, its historical context, its pertinence to modern
concerns, or how it has impacted me personally. Each
meditation concludes with a prayer, sometimes very brief,
arising from my reflecting on the hymn. Italicized passages in
quotation marks are my imaginings of words spoken by God or
Christ to me—to us.

All the hymns I have chosen for these meditations are old
ones. The two most recent, "Morning has broken" and "God
of grace and God of glory," were both written in the 1930s. It's
not that I don't enjoy singing more recent hymns. I do. But
many recent hymns are of a genre called "praise" or "renewal"
music. I like singing this music. As with nineteenth-century
gospel hymnody, which it resembles and which I also enjoy
singing, praise music moves the heart and is easy to learn,
making it useful in worship. But the texts are often repetitive
and rely on stock phrases. For me, they do not hold up well
when used for meditation.

Anyone with two or more hymnals at hand will quickly
discover that many hymns vary from one hymnal to
another. Hymnal editors often revise the text of a hymn, for
a variety of reasons. Entire stanzas may be deleted and not
all hymnal editors delete the same stanzas. I have researched
the original text of most of the hymns discussed in this book
and in a few cases have reinserted a stanza omitted in many
hymnals but which I find helpful.

Editors also change the wording of sentences and phrases.
Some changes are made to clarify what a text is meant to say;
the meaning of words changes with time, sometimes making

the original meaning unintelligible to later generations. Editors also revise hymn texts to correct what they deem to be questionable theology.

In recent decades, editors have sought to remove the hint of sexism from hymns by eliminating or minimizing the use of masculine terms and pronouns when referring to God and to humanity. In the texts as quoted in this book, I have usually used the newer, inclusive wording and have done a bit of rewriting myself along those lines, though I have occasionally returned to the original wording when I felt a revision compromised the text's meaning.

Eliminating sexist language in hymns is a dicey undertaking. There is no way entirely to abandon the use of masculine words with reference to God without creating other problems. As for pronouns, the traditional *he* can suggest that God is male, but *she* could suggest that God is female. *It* will not do because God is personal, and *they* is out because God is one. That exhausts the available pronouns. But we need a pronoun because refusing to use one leads to awkward, clumsy prose that distracts more than it inspires or informs. Modern hymnal editors have minimized their use of pronouns when referring to God, but when they feel compelled to use one, most use *he* because it is biblical and traditional. The terms *Father* and *Lord* used with reference to God can also be painful for those whose father or authority figure was absent or abusive. But in my opinion, no suitable substitute for *Father* and *Lord* as terms for God has been found. Continuing to use these terms, but sparingly, seems to me the least unsatisfactory policy.

One reader of an early draft of this manuscript commented that this approach seemed very traditional. I'm not sure whether she meant that as a compliment or a criticism, but I wouldn't disagree. It's not that I fear new ideas. It just takes me a while to embrace them, and in my prayers, out of which these meditations arise, I am a traditionalist through and through.

Another reader commented that there's a lot about me in this book. I don't think I'm a narcissist, but since these meditations come out of my praying, they could hardly be about anyone else. At one point I tried to minimize my use of first-person singular pronouns, but that seemed artificial and contrived, so I have left most of them in. I hope readers will connect with the issues I wrestle with in my praying. As children of God seeking peace, strength, comfort, and love, we stand on common ground.

**Richard H. Schmidt**
**Fairhope, Alabama**

# 1

# A MIGHTY FORTRESS IS OUR GOD

Martin Luther (1483-1546)                    Suggested tune: *Ein feste Burg*
tr. Frederic Henry Hedge (1805-1890)

*A mighty fortress is our God, a bulwark never failing;*
*Our helper he amid the flood of mortal ills prevailing:*
*for still our ancient foe doth seek to work us woe;*
*his craft and power are great, and armed with cruel hate,*
*on earth is not his equal.*

*Did we in our own strength confide, our striving would be losing;*
*were not the right man on our side, the man of God's own choosing.*
*Dost ask who that may be? Christ Jesus it is he;*
*Lord Sabaoth his Name, from age to age the same,*
*and he must win the battle.*

*And though this world with devils filled, should threaten to undo us,*
*we will not fear for God hath willed his truth to triumph through us.*
*The prince of darkness grim, we tremble not for him;*
*his rage we can endure, for lo! his doom is sure,*
*one little word shall fell him.*

*That word above all earthly powers, no thanks to them, abideth;*
*the Spirit and the gifts are ours through him who with us sideth:*
*let goods and kindred go, this mortal life also,*
*the body they may kill: God's truth abideth still,*
*his kingdom is forever.*

---

Martin Luther, the great German theologian and leader of the Protestant Reformation, believed in hymn singing. "The devil, the originator of sorrowful anxieties and restless troubles, flees before the sound of music," he said. Luther wrote both the words and the music for this hymn, which he based on Psalm 46: "God is our refuge and strength, a very present help in trouble."

*A mighty fortress is our God, a bulwark never failing;*
*Our helper he amid the flood of mortal ills prevailing:*
*for still our ancient foe doth seek to work us woe;*
*his craft and power are great, and armed with cruel hate,*
*on earth is not his equal.*

Countless Christians have drawn strength from this hymn's robust, sinewy images of divine strength. But who is this "ancient foe" who threatens us? While neither Satan nor any other cosmic foe is mentioned in Psalm 46, the psalm does refer to earthquakes, raging seas, and war. Luther personalizes these dangers in his hymn by calling them *der alt' böse Feind*, the angry old enemy, a meaning retained in our translation.

I'm not sure about that understanding. While the devil has a prominent place in classical Christian imagery, he doesn't appear as a cosmic figure until very late in the Bible. But if human experience on earth includes rebellious self-will, could the same be true in other dimensions of reality? The Book of Revelation (12:7) refers to war in heaven. Perhaps there really are rebellious celestial creatures vying for human souls on earth. Maybe C. S. Lewis's *The Screwtape Letters*, purporting to contain the correspondence from a senior devil to his subordinate trying to win a human soul for hell, isn't entirely fictitious after all.

*Did we in our own strength confide, our striving would be losing;*
*were not the right man on our side, the man of God's own choosing.*
*Dost ask who that may be? Christ Jesus it is he;*
*Lord Sabaoth his Name, from age to age the same,*
*and he must win the battle.*

We don't need an "ancient foe" to seek to work us woe, for we work plenty of woe ourselves, and nothing on earth seems able to quell the power of the temptations we gladly entertain. It seems just a short time ago that my tall frame, daily exercise regimen, and youthful vigor gave me a sense of being in control of things, certainly of my own life. I also confided in my own intelligence and personality. Everything revolved around me. I'm grateful that some of my plans have come to pass, but I now realize that other people and fortuitous timing had as much to do with that as I did. Other plans went belly up, often because I made foolish mistakes. When I confided in my own strength, my striving was losing.

One of the advantages of old age is that the temptation to confide in our own strength wanes as our strength diminishes. When merely to rise from a chair requires careful unbending and steadying, the foolishness of confiding in our own strength stares us in the face.

And of course the "right man" is on our side, "the man of God's own choosing," which is to say, not the man of our own choosing. Many of us are still learning to trust Jesus Christ,

Lord Sabaoth (Lord of power and might). His priorities and plans often diverge from those we would have devised, and we can be thankful for that. "He must win the battle."

*And though this world with devils filled, should threaten to undo us,*
*we will not fear for God hath willed his truth to triumph through us.*
*The prince of darkness grim, we tremble not for him;*
*his rage we can endure, for lo! his doom is sure,*
*one little word shall fell him.*

If Christ will speak just "one little word" to fell the devil, what will that one little word be? Perhaps Luther didn't mean that literally *one* little word would defeat the prince of darkness, but why not a single word? What's the word? I think I know.

Julian of Norwich laughed because she knew the devil was overcome. I would go further and say that laughter renders the devil impotent. When people start laughing at you not because you're telling a joke but because you've become a laughingstock, you might as well hang it up and go home. Your influence is shot, as in the Hans Christian Andersen story: Only when the child laughed at the emperor's nakedness were the emperor's puffed-up pretensions exposed.

Alcoholics Anonymous meetings are full of laughter. These men and women have met the devil and walked the devil's path. But at some point (and most would say it was through divine intervention, often obliquely referred to as one's "Higher Power"), they were moved to turn a corner and head in a different direction. Their formerly humiliating and destructive behaviors, their once bloated egos and self-assertions, have now become funny stories. What once threatened their very lives has been reduced to a memory and a joke.

What one little word will Jesus speak to defeat the prince of darkness? I think it is "Ha!" I think Jesus will laugh in the devil's face.

> *That word above all earthly powers, no thanks to them, abideth;*
> *the Spirit and the gifts are ours through him who with us sideth:*
> *let goods and kindred go, this mortal life also,*
> *the body they may kill: God's truth abideth still,*
> *his kingdom is forever.*

The question is not whether we will "let goods and kindred go, this mortal life also"—we will let them go, like it or not. The question is whether we will do so indignantly, grasping for control even as it slips from us, or humbly and confident that "God's truth abideth still, his kingdom is forever." I've seen it happen both ways. Those who have never learned to trust God or anyone else and have unresolved conflicts and troubled relationships usually pass from this life tense and angry. They make life miserable to the very end for family, friends, clergy, and care providers who seek to care for and minister to them. But those who have surrendered and accepted "the Spirit and the gifts" that "are ours through him who with us sideth" are often able to die gratefully and become a blessing to those around them.

## ⊶⊷ PRAYER ⊶⊷

When I read the morning paper or watch the evening news, I often find it difficult to trust you, Lord. The news usually tells of war, famine, oppression, disease, homelessness, and acts of corruption or violence against the innocent by selfish or angry people. The prince of darkness grim seems to be running rampant these days. It's a leap of faith not to tremble for him. I want to take that leap of faith, Lord, and some days I do. But then the next day, there's another bombing or shooting. It's all so confusing and disheartening.

I remember a comment by Desmond Tutu, who won the Nobel Peace Prize for his work in dismantling apartheid and seeking reconciliation. He said, "We prayed that God would bless our land and would confound the machinations of the children of darkness. There had been so many moments in the past, during the dark days of apartheid's vicious awfulness, when we had preached, 'This is God's world and God is in charge!' When evil seemed to be on the rampage and about to overwhelm goodness, we held on to this article of faith by the skin of our teeth. It was a kind of theological whistling in the dark and we were frequently tempted to whisper in God's ear, 'For goodness sake, why don't you make it more obvious that *you are* in charge?'" That's a question I would like to ask you right now, Lord.

Be our fortress, and not ours only. Shelter all your endangered children—Christians, Jews, Muslims, atheists, people who have never heard of you or given you a thought. You are the God of us all. Speak that one little word to defeat Satan and his minions, and let us hear you speak it!

And then, dear Lord, hold us in your arms. Yes, we need you to be our fortress, our refuge, our strength, for of ourselves we are weak and wearied. But a fortress is hard and stony. We need more than your strength. We need you to be soft as well as strong. Hold us in your lap as a mother holds her child. Let us feel your warmth and hear the beating of your heart. After taking us into your castle, hug us and hum in our ears one of the songs of heaven. Let us know not only that you protect us but also that you protect us because you love us.

*Amen.*

# 2

## ABIDE WITH ME

Henry Francis Lyte (1793-1847)          Suggested tune: *Eventide*

*Abide with me; fast falls the eventide;*
*the darkness deepens; Lord, with me abide.*
*When other helpers fail and comforts flee,*
*help of the helpless, O abide with me.*

*Swift to its close ebbs out life's little day;*
*earth's joys grow dim; its glories pass away;*
*change and decay in all around I see;*
*O thou who changest not, abide with me.*

*Thou on my head in early youth didst smile;*
*and, though rebellious and perverse a while,*
*thou hast not left me, oft as I left thee.*
*On to the close, O Lord, abide with me.*

*I need thy presence every passing hour.*
*What but thy grace can foil the tempter's power?*
*Who, like thyself, my guide and stay can be?*
*Through cloud and sunshine, Lord, abide with me.*

*I fear no foe, with thee at hand to bless;*
*ills have no weight, and tears no bitterness.*
*Where is death's sting? Where, grave, thy victory?*
*I triumph still, if thou abide with me.*

*Hold thou thy cross before my closing eyes;*
*shine through the gloom and point me to the skies.*
*Heaven's morning breaks, and earth's vain shadows flee.*
*In life, in death, O Lord, abide with me.*

This hymn is based on John 15:1-11. It uses the fading light
of dusk as a metaphor for approaching death. Henry Francis
Lyte, who also wrote "Praise, my soul, the King of heaven"
(See Hymn #35), was born in Scotland but served for years
as a priest in a fishing village on the Devonshire coast. There
is some question about when the hymn was written. Lyte may
have written it following the death of a friend or, never in
good health himself, when his own strength began to fail at
the end of his life. *Eventide* is one of many hymn settings
by the distinguished nineteenth-century choirmaster and
hymnal editor William Henry Monk.

*Abide with me; fast falls the eventide;*
*the darkness deepens; Lord, with me abide.*
*When other helpers fail and comforts flee,*
*help of the helpless, O abide with me.*

The Greek verb *meno* (abide) suggests an intentional,
continuing, long-term habitation or relationship. One does
not "abide" in a hotel room, a parking space, the checkout
line, or an elevator. Home is where we abide. It is the

backdrop of our lives, an atmosphere that we breathe in and out. Filled with our own memories and mementos, tailored to our needs and desires, home surrounds and defines us.

Home is also a place we don't have to think about all the time. Abiding at home affords us the security and freedom to think about other things. We will clean, cook, eat, wash, pay the bills, run errands, raise our children, brush our teeth, pick up our clothes, read the paper, entertain friends, make a living, make the bed, make amends, make love, make do.

As we abide with Christ and he with us, many other things will occupy our minds. It is neither necessary nor helpful to think or talk about Jesus all the time—so long as he abides with us. Christ invites us to make our home with him so that he might surround and define us and condition all we say or do, hallowing every moment. He wishes to come not to sojourn or visit but to settle in and remain, through thick and thin, good times and bad, straight through to the end and beyond. Christ would be our familiar place, the backdrop of our lives, the air we breathe, enfolding and embracing us.

> *Swift to its close ebbs out life's little day;*
> *earth's joys grow dim; its glories pass away;*
> *change and decay in all around I see;*
> *O thou who changest not, abide with me.*

Though this hymn was often sung at the church where my family worshiped, it meant little to me growing up, and as a young priest, I rarely chose it for a worship service. Perhaps I was too busy checking calendars, going places, and doing things to give thought to abiding anywhere. But now as the eventide of my life is at hand, this text has new power for me.

As for earth's joys and glories, I've had more than my share, and I know that like sparks from a campfire, they do not last. A century from now, no one will remember me or perhaps even know my name. If my books are still found on library shelves, they will be dusty from having sat there untouched for years.

It is not necessary that future generations remember any of us. What would be the point? New generations must meet their own challenges, not obsess about how we did or did not meet ours. Let us appreciate earth's joys and glories for what they are—quickly fading pleasures to be enjoyed but not clung to. But Christ abides with us even when all else has passed away.

As the darkness deepens, I am discovering that it need not terrify. When my mind and body are no longer agile and I am no longer sought after, when I must depend on the kindness of others, I shall try to unclench my fists, let go of everything, trust the grace I have experienced so many times before, and look to Christ to abide with me. When I depart this life, may I go gently and confidently into that good night because the help of the helpless abides with me.

> Thou on my head in early youth didst smile;
> and, though rebellious and perverse a while,
> thou hast not left me, oft as I left thee.
> On to the close, O Lord, abide with me.

As a youth, I was not outwardly "rebellious and perverse." My rebellion and perversity were subtler. I cultivated the socially acceptable persona that would allow me to play the role of good little boy, and then later, biblical scholar, spiritual guide, and respected arbiter of truth and falsehood. Oh, the places I'd go, the things I'd do! I once undertook to read the entire New Testament every month—about ten chapters a day—but not in order to draw closer to God. I wanted to impress people with my ability to quote scripture from memory. All the while I was drifting farther and farther from God because I worshiped an idol, namely myself.

Perhaps God smiled on me in those days. Many a youth has entertained similarly grand dreams. Such grandiosity may even be a necessary stage in growing up. God probably knew I'd run into a wall before long and get the sense knocked into me, and then I'd invite him to abide with me on very different terms.

> I need thy presence every passing hour.
> What but thy grace can foil the tempter's power?
> Who, like thyself, my guide and stay can be?
> Through cloud and sunshine, Lord, abide with me.

Yes, every passing hour. We don't need to be thinking pious thoughts every passing hour, but even when other things claim our attention, and even in moments of doubt and disbelief, we need Christ's presence in our souls. I used to fight my doubts, but I no longer do because it accomplishes nothing. The doubts don't go away, so I have signed a truce with them. They are permitted to remain but not to trouble me. They will not command my attention. I think of my doubts as spiritual mosquitos, a nuisance I can live with. And the continuing presence of doubt still leaves plenty of room in my mind for Christ to abide there as well. I focus on him. In the words of Annie S. Hawks's gospel hymn, "I need thee every hour, stay thou nearby; temptations lose their power when thou art nigh."

> *I fear no foe, with thee at hand to bless;*
> *ills have no weight, and tears no bitterness.*
> *Where is death's sting? Where, grave, thy victory?*
> *I triumph still, if thou abide with me.*

It's still a leap for me to "fear no foe." Ills still have weight for me, and I can still cry bitter tears. I am still learning to trust the One who has been so good to me in the past. Some days, the lesson seems fairly well learned; other days, it seems I've never heard of it. But for all that, for all my slipping and stumbling along the way, "I triumph still, if thou abide with me."

> *Hold thou thy cross before my closing eyes;*
> *shine through the gloom and point me to the skies.*
> *Heaven's morning breaks, and earth's vain shadows flee.*
> *In life, in death, O Lord, abide with me.*

The final stanza of this hymn is the prayer of someone at the point of death. Our advancing helplessness, pondered in the previous stanzas, is about to culminate in a final act of surrender. Many of us grow anxious as we see death approaching. It is the end of everything we know. It is so final. But death is also the beginning of something not yet known but promised to be glorious, and the hymn points to that as well. As heaven's morning breaks, Jesus Christ shines through the gloom and points us to the skies. Our experience of Christ this side of death suggests what awaits us on the other side: Failure and defeat are not our final destination but way stations on the road to glory.

 ## PRAYER

When I depart this life and enter that good night, Lord Jesus, cleanse me, hold me close, and make for me a place where I may gaze at last upon your face. I do not now ask that you do anything. You have already done many things well for me. Nor do I ask that you enable me to do anything. I have already done much, some of it well, some of it poorly, some of it of

no consequence. My time of doing has passed. I ask only that you abide with me. Sit with me. Listen to the sounds that I hear and breathe the air that I breathe. When I open my eyes, may I see some indication of your presence. In the middle of the night, may I hear your voice. When I grow restless, hold my hand. In life, in death, O thou who changest not, abide with me.

*Amen.*

# 3

# AH, HOLY JESUS

Johann Heermann (1585-1647)          Suggested tune: *Herzliebster Jesu*
tr. Robert Seymour Bridges (1844-1930)

Ah, holy Jesus, how hast thou offended,
that man to judge thee hath in hate pretended?
By foes derided, by thine own rejected,
O most afflicted.

Who was the guilty? Who brought this upon thee?
Alas, my treason, Jesus, hath undone thee.
'Twas I, Lord Jesus, I it was denied thee:
I crucified thee.

Lo, the Good Shepherd for the sheep is offered;
the slave hath sinned, and the Son hath suffered;
for our atonement, while we nothing heeded,
God interceded.

For me, kind Jesus, was thy incarnation,
thy mortal sorrow, and thy life's oblation;
thy death of anguish and thy bitter passion,
for my salvation.

Therefore, kind Jesus, since I cannot pay thee,
I do adore thee, and will ever pray thee,
think on thy pity and thy love unswerving,
not my deserving.

Personal and family tragedies led the Austrian Lutheran pastor Johann Heermann to reflect on the sufferings of Christ. Originally fifteen stanzas in length and based on biblical, Latin, and German sources, Heermann's hymn is an intensely personal confession and meditation on the atonement. The solemn, pensive tune *Herzliebster Jesu*, based on earlier melodies, was composed by the German composer Johann Crüger and published in 1640.

*Ah, holy Jesus, how hast thou offended,*
*that man to judge thee hath in hate pretended?*
*By foes derided, by thine own rejected,*
*O most afflicted.*

How did it come to this, Jesus? It started with such promise: the lame walked, lepers were cleansed, the blind saw, demons were cast out, and crowds gathered to listen as you opened the scriptures to them. I followed you along those Galilean roads. It was all so happy. How did it come to this?

It may have started downhill with your words on the mountain, "You have heard that it was said such and such, but I say to you so and so." You didn't merely open the scriptures—you blew them open and became your own scripture. You grabbed the scriptures by the neck and dragged them to a place no one had imagined. Who would have expected anyone to say what you said and do what you did? Indiscreet? Presumptuous? Radical? Lawless? Blasphemous? Many thought so.

Even your own turned away from you, and I was one of them. It wasn't that I didn't love you, Jesus, but I didn't realize what I had signed on for; I was frightened. So I fled. That's what frightened people do.

*Who was the guilty? Who brought this upon thee?*
*Alas, my treason, Jesus, hath undone thee.*
*'Twas I, Lord Jesus, I it was denied thee:*
*I crucified thee.*

"Who was the guilty? Who brought this upon thee?" Who? No, Lord! I didn't join in the jeering and the catcalls. I was appalled by it. But what could I, a mere bystander, have done? I couldn't have stopped it. It was a mob scene. My standing beside you or seeking to intervene would have changed nothing. The rioters wouldn't have listened to me.

You say none of that mattered? That you were looking not for results but for faithfulness? But what use is faithfulness without results? I am not a traitor. A traitor turns against his friends. I didn't turn against you, Lord. I was always for you. I didn't do anything.

*"Yes, exactly. You did nothing. It didn't matter to me that your speaking out wouldn't have quelled the mob. What would have mattered was your doing or saying something, anything, to let me know you were with me and would stay with me to the end, that you loved me as I love you. Your doing nothing drove a nail not into my hands, but into my heart. Alas, your treason has undone me. 'Twas you, you it was denied me: you crucified me."*

*Lo, the Good Shepherd for the sheep is offered;*
*the slave hath sinned, and the Son hath suffered;*
*for our atonement, while we nothing heeded,*
*God interceded.*

Meanwhile, you, the Good Shepherd, offered yourself for me
and for all of us, your lost sheep. Meanwhile, you suffered "for
our atonement." Meanwhile, "God interceded." It wasn't about
us so much as it was about you. You did not stop offering,
suffering, and interceding until our atonement was complete,
and now that it is complete, you invite us to take our place in
your arms, the arms of our Good Shepherd, never again to slip
from your embrace. I'm coming, Lord Jesus.

*For me, kind Jesus, was thy incarnation,*
*thy mortal sorrow, and thy life's oblation;*
*thy death of anguish and thy bitter passion,*
*for my salvation.*

The hardest thing to accept, Lord Jesus, is that you died for
me, for my salvation. I can possibly believe that you would
assume human flesh and die a death of "bitter passion" for
someone or something else: for good people, or suffering
people, or repentant sinners, or innocent victims. Or for
humanity in general, created in your image but gone off
track. Or for the planet itself, that shining blue sphere that
you made and pronounced good but that we are despoiling.
A loving God might, conceivably, die for that. But for me?
Me personally? Me specifically? It feels presumptuous
and blasphemous even to think it. Appearing before you,
I can only see myself covering my head, crawling beneath
something, and whispering, "Miserere! Mercy!"

*"Stop it right now! I am sick of your misereres. It was fine for you to ask for mercy at first, but I'm telling you I've granted it, so stop asking for it. Yes, I died on the cross for all those other people and for the planet, but I also did it for you, personally and specifically for you. You can say thank you, but you needn't say it over and over for all eternity. My greatest joy will be to see you laughing and dancing and singing as my beloved, with an unburdened heart in the mansion I have prepared for you. Don't wait a moment longer."*

> Therefore, kind Jesus, since I cannot pay thee,
> I do adore thee, and will ever pray thee,
> think on thy pity and thy love unswerving,
> not my deserving.

Well then! How can I pay you? I like to earn what I get and get what I earn. So if I cannot earn your kindness in advance, tell me how I can pay you for it after the fact.

*"It's paid in full. The nail prints in my hands are the receipt."*

Ah! "Therefore, kind Jesus, since I cannot pay thee, I do adore thee, and will ever pray thee." Adoration and prayer. That's all I can offer.

*"And it's all I want from you."*

## ⸺ ⸙ ⸺ PRAYER ⸺ ⸙ ⸺

Holy Jesus, I've never understood the atonement. Yes, God is holy and almighty, and I am sinful and rebellious. That creates an abyss between us that I'm keenly aware of. But I don't understand how your dying so long ago bridged that abyss. If you paid my debt, how did that work exactly? To whom did you pay it? I've read all the classical theories about the atonement, but they go right over my head.

One thing I do understand, though. What you did for me, holy Jesus, you did while I was not paying attention, occupied with other things, heeding nothing. I had studied the Bible and preached many a sermon, but I was busy running a parish and a publishing company, writing books and articles, planning meetings and retreats. Others were busy making and selling things, traveling, entertaining, or competing for this or that prize. We all had jobs to do, people to meet, places to go. I had forgotten why I did any of it yet kept doing it anyway. I was wandering in the wilderness and didn't know it. I was a slave but thought I was free. And sometimes not much seems to have changed even today.

I suppose that's enough for me to understand. Now I have sat up and noticed. Now I thank you, holy Jesus; I simply and merely thank you. Instruct, discipline, and nurture me, my Good Shepherd, until I become your good sheep, worthy to bear your name and rest in your arms.

*"Understanding isn't necessary. It's a vain fancy. Forget it. Faithfulness is all that matters. That's what I long to see in you."*

*Amen.*

**4**

# ALLELUIA! SING TO JESUS!

William Chatterton Dix (1837-1898)                    Suggested tune: *Hyfrydol*

*Alleluia! Sing to Jesus! His the scepter, his the throne.*
*Alleluia! His the triumph, his the victory alone.*
*Hark! The songs of peaceful Zion thunder like a mighty flood;*
*Jesus out of every nation hath redeemed us by his blood.*

*Alleluia! Not as orphans are we left in sorrow now.*
*Alleluia! He is with us, faith believes nor questions how:*
*though the cloud from sight received him,*
      *when the forty days were o'er,*
*shall our hearts forget his promise, "I am with you evermore"?*

*Alleluia! Bread of heaven, thou on earth our food, our stay!*
*Alleluia! Here the sinful flee to thee from day to day.*
*Intercessor, friend of sinners, earth's Redeemer, plead for me,*
*where the songs of all the sinless sweep across the crystal sea.*

*Alleluia! King eternal, thee the Lord of lords we own.*
*Alleluia! Born of Mary, earth thy footstool, heaven thy throne.*
*Thou within the veil hast entered,*
      *robed in flesh, our great high priest:*
*thou on earth both priest and victim in the eucharistic feast.*

This hymn is based on Revelation 5:9: "They sing a new
song: 'You are worthy to take the scroll and to open its seals,
for you were slaughtered and by your blood you ransomed
for God saints from every tribe and language and people and
nation.'" William Chatterton Dix was an English insurance
company manager. *Hyfryrdol* was written by a Welshman,
Rowland Hugh Prichard, and was first published in 1855.
"Love divine, all loves excelling" and other texts have been
set to it as well.

---

*Alleluia! Sing to Jesus! His the scepter, his the throne.*
*Alleluia! His the triumph, his the victory alone.*
*Hark! The songs of peaceful Zion thunder like a mighty flood;*
*Jesus out of every nation hath redeemed us by his blood.*

Orthodox and medieval iconographers often depict the
risen Christ seated on a throne holding an orb in his
hand. In November, at the end of the liturgical year,
Roman Catholics observe the feast of Christ the King
and Protestants sing "Crown him with many crowns, the
Lamb upon his throne." Christians of all sorts worship a
triumphant, monarchial Christ.

Jesus of Nazareth didn't deny he was a king but said his
kingship was "not from this world" (John 18:36). So far as
this world goes, Jesus was a humble carpenter and itinerant
preacher and healer in an obscure province of the Roman
Empire who never traveled far from home. It's quite a leap
from that to Christus Rex. How did this leap occur?

It started in the fourth century when the Emperor
Constantine converted to Christianity and made it the state
religion of the Roman Empire. Bishops donned regal attire
and became imperial advisors; huge basilicas were built; the
church became a major power broker. Even hermit monks
who shunned earthly power and pleasures worshiped Christ
as King. But what kind of king?

*Alleluia! Not as orphans are we left in sorrow now.*
*Alleluia! He is with us, faith believes nor questions how:*
*though the cloud from sight received him,*
    *when the forty days were o'er,*
*shall our hearts forget his promise, "I am with you evermore"?*

I cherish the thought that when I walk through the valley
of the shadow of death, a walk I know awaits me, I shall
not walk alone, as an orphan, because of Christ's promise
"I am with you evermore." How Christ will bring this to
pass, I don't know, and even if it were explained to me, I
would probably still not grasp it. Confusion and lack of
understanding seem part of my essential identity. But faith
isn't a matter of knowing how God achieves his ends but of
trusting God's promise. Perhaps because understanding is
beyond me, I am reduced to trusting promises. May I do
it contentedly, never holding out for an understanding I
cannot have and do not need.

*Alleluia! Bread of heaven, thou on earth our food, our stay!*
*Alleluia! Here the sinful flee to thee from day to day.*
*Intercessor, friend of sinners, earth's Redeemer, plead for me,*
*where the songs of all the sinless sweep across the crystal sea.*

If by bread we mean a food made of flour, water, and yeast, then the phrase "bread of heaven" is nonsense. But if bread can also represent something beyond human understanding, the phrase may point to a reality our language lacks words for.

An experience years ago helped me see what this may mean. I was in a music store looking through phonograph records (that tells you how long ago this was) when I came across a recording of Franz Liszt's solo piano transcription of the *Symphonie Fantastique* by Hector Berlioz. It seems that before the days of phonographs, Liszt made piano transcriptions of several symphonies to enable persons with access only to a piano to experience the symphony. The sound would be different, but the notes would be the same.

I bought the record and played it. In the limited medium of the piano, a single note represented many different orchestral sounds. I imagined how someone who knew only of the piano might respond if I said that a particular note on the piano represented a bolder sound played by the brass section and that another represented a softer, smoother sound played by the strings. "You're talking nonsense!" he might say. "A note is a note, period! There are no such things as brass and strings."

If God sought to offer heavenly nourishment—a reality beyond human understanding—in the limited medium of human experience, he might do it with bread (or wine, water, or any other ordinary thing). To call this nonsense would say more about our small minds than about what God was doing. Christ commanded us to take and eat, not to take and understand. Some things are more than they seem.

*Alleluia! King eternal, thee the Lord of lords we own.*
*Alleluia! Born of Mary, earth thy footstool, heaven thy throne.*
*Thou within the veil hast entered,*
*    robed in flesh, our great high priest:*
*thou on earth both priest and victim in the eucharistic feast.*

This stanza picks up where the first stanza left off. What kind
of king do we worship? "King eternal, thee the Lord of lords
we own" is a line Jews, Christians, and Muslims alike could
sing. But what comes next is uniquely Christian. Christians
pledge allegiance to a monarch who rules through benevolent
humility rather than by conquest. Only Christians believe that
the King eternal, the Lord of lords, the omnipotent Creator
of the universe, was born of a human mother, assumed human
flesh, lived a human life, and died a human death. Muslims in
particular regard this notion as a scandalous affront to God.

But this is how we Christians experience God—not as someone
reigning high above but as someone stooping to serve. Heaven
may be his throne, but earth is his footstool. He stands where
we stand. The Creator God has entered the veil, an image
suggesting the obscure, cloudy quality of much of human life;
he is robed in flesh, subjecting himself to every human frailty.
It is a kind of kingship unknown among human rulers.

Jesus is qualified to act as "our great high priest" because of
his humility. This is discussed at length in the New Testament
Epistle to the Hebrews. A priest is a mediator, a go-between
linking God and humanity, bridging the abyss between us.
That is who Jesus Christ was and is, and after him no further
priests are needed. Those who (like me) carry the title of
priest do so only because we're stand-ins for Christ. It's not a
matter of who we are, but of who he is.

## PRAYER

Lord Jesus, I haven't forgotten your promise "I am with you evermore," but there is a persistent little voice in the back of my head that pooh-poohs your promise. I first heard that voice in college, when I began reading authors who sought to debunk the faith I had brought with me from my childhood. That faith may have been naïve, even childish in some ways, but it strengthened and comforted me, and I grieved its loss. I still do. My faith today is probably more mature, but I liked my old faith better.

"Faith believes nor questions how." That's my problem, Jesus. I question everything. I want to know how, to accept only what can be proven, and whatever else can be said of faith, you can't prove it. If you could, it wouldn't be faith; it would be knowledge, like the multiplication table or the recipe for cornbread. Knowledge is useful, but there's no mystery or joy in it, and it calls for no commitment or risk taking. I accept that, but if it isn't too much to ask, Lord, could you occasionally give me a glimpse of your face that lies beyond doubt, something that skeptical little voice within me cannot scoff at?

You have assured me that you are for me, pleading my case. I pray to you daily and convey to you my hopes and fears, my thanksgivings and requests, but my prayers can be perfunctory and my mind is often elsewhere. Intercept my prayers, Lord, and then edit, refine, and expand them until they become the prayers I should be praying, until they become your prayers. Then please sign my name to them and forward them on to that place "where the songs of all the sinless sweep across the crystal sea."

Is it too much to envision myself among those sinless souls singing songs that sweep across that crystal sea? I imagine my songs, as refined by you, Lord Jesus, harmonizing with the voices of the four living creatures singing, "Holy! Holy! Holy!" and the myriads of angels singing, "Worthy is the Lamb that was slain to receive power and wealth and wisdom and might and honor and glory and blessing!"

I know better than to take those images literally. They were all dreamt by a Jewish mystic on a Greek island two thousand years ago (Revelation 4–5). That means they are symbolic, as dreams always are. What do they symbolize? Even if I were shown it, Lord Jesus, I doubt I would understand the thousandth part of it. It is not for me to understand but to sing and adore, and when my singing and my adoration fall short, I trust that you, Lord Jesus, will make them what they should be.

*Amen.*

# 5

# AMAZING GRACE

John Newton (1725-1807), stanzas 1-4          Suggested tune: *New Britain*
Anonymous, stanza 5

Amazing grace! How sweet the sound
that saved a wretch like me!
I once was lost but now am found,
was blind but now I see.

'Twas grace that taught my heart to fear,
and grace my fears relieved;
how precious did that grace appear
the hour I first believed.

The Lord has promised good to me,
his word my hope secures;
he will my shield and portion be
as long as life endures.

Through many dangers, toils, and snares,
I have already come;
'tis grace that brought me safe thus far,
and grace will lead me home.

When we've been there ten thousand years,
bright shining as the sun,
we've no less days to sing God's praise
than when we'd first begun.

The story of John Newton's life has inspired millions. His tombstone in the parish churchyard in Olney, England, bears this inscription: "John Newton, Clerk [clergyman], once an Infidel and Libertine, a servant of slaves in Africa, was, by the rich mercy of our Lord and Saviour Jesus Christ, preserved, restored, pardoned, and appointed to preach the Faith he had long laboured to destroy." The earliest known use of the tune *New Britain* was in a shape-note songbook published by Benjamin Shaw and Charles H. Spilman in 1829.

*Amazing grace! How sweet the sound*
*that saved a wretch like me!*
*I once was lost but now am found,*
*was blind but now I see.*

Popular as this hymn has become in recent years, some dislike referring to themselves as wretches. "I'm not a wretch!" they insist. Well, that depends on what you mean by wretch. If a wretch is someone who wastes his life in unbridled self-indulgence, moral depravity, and preying off the innocent, then few people are wretches. But if a wretch is someone who has lost his way and is trapped in a thicket of briars and poisonous plants, then I've been there and so have many others. I refer to spiritual thickets, to briars and poisonous plants like resentment, boredom, indifference, anger, and self-absorption. That's a pretty good description of the soul of an addict. I was trapped in such a thicket myself until, in 1983, I went to my first Alcoholics Anonymous meeting.

That's also when this hymn, which I had previously regarded as overly sentimental, sprang to life for me. In fact, the entire Christian gospel, about which I'd been preaching for more than a decade, became real for me as if for the first time. The gospel story became my story. I realized that this hymn and the Bible were talking about my own life. Wretch is not too strong a word to describe what I was. I had been lost, but now I was found.

This was through no act of my own. Someone had sought me out, found me, revived me, pumped me up again, and given me a fresh start. And I know who it was. Now I see.

*'Twas grace that taught my heart to fear,*
*and grace my fears relieved;*
*how precious did that grace appear*
*the hour I first believed.*

Although I refer to addiction and recovery several times in these pages, those references do not comprise the main thrust of these meditations. But I cannot sing "Amazing grace" without reliving my recovery and my stunning discovery that grace—God's unmerited love for the lost—is for real.

Fear was part of that grace. I was terrified during the final months of my drinking. Unable to control my addiction, I feared I would lose my family, my job, my savings, my health, and my life. I envisioned myself tottering on the brink of a precipice, staring down at jagged boulders hundreds of feet below. At any moment, I could trip and fall to my death. It was that fear that drove me to walk into my first Alcoholics Anonymous meeting. There, to my great surprise and relief,

I was embraced by loving, understanding friends. I soon came to see them as divine agents.

The fear that drove me into recovery was as much an act of divine grace as my recovery itself. "'Twas grace that taught my heart to fear," for without the fear, I would never have walked into that meeting, and I would be dead today. Those who remember me would be shaking their heads and saying, "What a shame. What a waste."

But that was not to be. God had other plans for me. I have no doubt fallen short of what God envisioned for me, but it is only by God's grace that I have been able to be and to do anything at all.

> The Lord has promised good to me,
> his word my hope secures;
> he will my shield and portion be
> as long as life endures.

"His word" could refer to the Bible, but I take it to mean the divine Word or *logos* who entered the world and assumed human flesh, full of grace and truth (John 1). The Bible testifies to him, but one could conceivably know the Word made flesh without ever having heard of the Bible. It is Jesus Christ who secures our hope.

Many Christians know their hope is secure, and they don't doubt it. Christ's presence in their souls gives them that "blessed assurance." I wish I were one of those Christians. My hope may be secure, but my sense of it isn't. I wonder about every article of my faith. Bad things happen to people, innocent people. Why is that? Is God really in charge? What

if our hope is in vain? I can't entirely shoo these questions
away. God's goodness may be the foundation on which the
universe rests, but my hope of it is feeble and tottering. I'm
thankful that the story that culminates in Jesus includes many
chapters showing God to be the "shield and portion" even of
those whose faith is a dimly burning wick.

> *Through many dangers, toils, and snares,*
> *I have already come;*
> *'tis grace that brought me safe thus far,*
> *and grace will lead me home.*

Inability to control my drinking was perhaps the most
outwardly noticeable of the "dangers, toils, and snares"
through which I have come, but it was also a symptom of a
deeper, less visible malady: I thought everything revolved
around me, my ideas and plans. I placed myself at the center
of my universe, defining everyone and everything else as it
pertained to me. God was somewhere in that mix, but when I
thought of God, it was about God's relationship to me; I was
still at the center.

Ensnared in the sin of pride even as I went about doing
God's work, I was in a dangerous place. So subtle was it that
for years I didn't recognize it. It took an act of divine grace
to bring me to my senses, and it wasn't fun. Acts of grace
are often not pleasant experiences because they disabuse us
of delusions we have come to treasure. Seeing myself as the
center of things made me feel important and powerful. I
liked that. But then my legs were knocked out from under
me—an act of grace—and I accepted the truth that God does
not need me. God and God's world have gotten along for

eons without me and will get along for eons without me after I'm gone.

We are but waves on the seashore, puffs of wind in the air. But God knows who we are and the grace that has brought us safe thus far will also lead us home. It's about God, not about us.

> *When we've been there ten thousand years,*
> *bright shining as the sun,*
> *we've no less days to sing God's praise*
> *than when we'd first begun.*

As a child, I thought of eternity as endless time—an extension of this life or something like it but with no death at the end. Later I came to see time as having a beginning and an end, like a yardstick, with my life occurring somewhere on that continuum, and God looking down at the entire yardstick from above it, taking in all of time at a glance. That second idea still envisioned eternity in terms of time—at the end of the yardstick something else would come, possibly a new yardstick or a different kind of measurement. This anonymous fifth stanza, usually sung as the concluding stanza of John Newton's hymn, envisions eternity that way. That shouldn't surprise us, since all human experience occurs within the context of time, and timelessness is a concept impossible for us to grasp.

But eternity is outside of time. Like all created things, time will someday come to an end. Then what? Would the Word then mean anything at that point? When Buddhists and Hindus ponder eternity, they assume that individual identity, integral to life within time, will be dissolved, rather as a drop of water is dissolved in the sea. But Western faith traditions, including Judaism, Christianity, and Islam, teach that God, having created individuals, does not uncreate us but redeems us, welcoming us into eternity with our individual identities intact but transformed.

We cannot understand this, but our experience of divine grace in this life should inform our thoughts of such things. If grace has brought us safe thus far, grace will lead us home, whatever home may be.

## PRAYER

How do I thank you, O God, for a life so filled with grace, with blessings undeserved? I have made so many stupid, vain decisions—I can't imagine why you came to me and lifted me out of the pit I was digging for myself. Nor can I imagine why you continue to come to me when I still make stupid, vain decisions. I say I want to be your man, but then...well, I don't have to tell you the rest of it. But you do not abandon me. You embrace me again and again. How do I thank you, O God?

*Amen.*

# 6

# BE THOU MY VISION

Irish, ca. 700
tr. by Eleanor H. Hull (1860-1935)

Suggested tune: *Slane*

Be thou my vision, O Lord of my heart;
all else be nought to me, save that thou art—
thou my best thought, by day or by night,
waking or sleeping, thy presence my light.

Be thou my wisdom, and thou my true word;
I ever with thee and thou with me, Lord;
thou my great Father; thine own may I be;
thou in me dwelling, and I one with thee.

High King of heaven, when victory is won,
may I reach heaven's joys, bright heaven's sun!
Heart of my heart, whatever befall,
still be my vision, O Ruler of all.

The ancient Celts had a strong sense of the presence of
danger, both physical and spiritual, and of Christ as the
shield to protect them. This hymn is an abbreviated version
of an ancient Celtic *lorica*. Loricas were hymns sung to
invoke Christ's protection. *Slane* is a traditional Irish
melody.

————— ∞∞∞ —————

*Be thou my vision, O Lord of my heart;*
*all else be nought to me, save that thou art—*
*thou my best thought, by day or by night,*
*waking or sleeping, thy presence my light.*

As I began to think about what it might mean for the Lord
to be my vision, I was interrupted by a telephone call from
Tommy. Tommy is in his sixties. I knew Tommy forty years
ago but then lost track of him. But a decade ago, Tommy
learned where I was living and telephoned me out of the
blue. He has been calling me about once a month ever since.
Tommy is mentally challenged. His father died three years
ago, and Tommy now lives alone, confined to his apartment.
He walks with a walker. He tells me most people avoid making
eye contact with him. My conversations with Tommy are
always the same—I listen as he talks about his loneliness,
his love of puppies, his literary ambitions, his theories on
astral projection, and his caregiver's impatience with him.
I like to think that our conversations bring a few moments
of affirmation to Tommy's life. When I visualize Tommy in
my mind, I try to see him as God sees him, precious and
beloved. "Be thou my vision, O Lord of my heart."

*Be thou my wisdom, and thou my true word;*
*I ever with thee and thou with me, Lord;*
*thou my great Father; thine own may I be;*
*thou in me dwelling, and I one with thee.*

Part of wisdom is acknowledging that what we know amounts to nothing. Wisdom is not understanding great things but embracing our natural condition, including our ignorance. We can pretend to have answers to life's deepest questions but that won't change anything except to cause us to appear grandiose and foolish and perhaps lose some friends. We understand God least of all. How can the human mind begin to grasp what or who God is? When we think of God, we get hints of God's reality at best, and even of those hints our understanding is surely flawed.

Embracing my ignorance doesn't depress me. Rather, I find it hugely liberating and I thank God for revealing it to me. How freeing to acknowledge that I am not expected to solve even the minor mysteries of living, much less the mystery of God! What a burden they must carry who set out to do that.

I believe God created all of us ignorant and loves us that way. I also believe that we need not experience our ignorance as darkness because God has come to us in the person of Jesus Christ. If we want to know who God is, or at least all we need to know about who God is, we need look no further than there. The deepest wisdom is to know Jesus Christ and to let him remake us into his likeness. Everything else is beyond our capacity. Let it go.

> High King of heaven, when victory is won,
> may I reach heaven's joys, bright heaven's sun!
> Heart of my heart, whatever befall,
> still be my vision, O Ruler of all.

God surely knows when his victory will be won, but I don't look for it soon. The world seems like a sordid mess these days. Perhaps it always seems that way. God's victory seems as far off now as ever, possibly further off. Sometimes God himself seems far off.

But I try not to obsess over what I cannot fix, and I don't try to banish the uncertainties that flit through my mind. I can accept them. Though I understand little or nothing, often can't discern even the outskirts of God's ways and may be contributing unwittingly to the evils I abhor, I ask God to solder my heart to his. "Whatever befall, still be my vision, O Ruler of all."

And then, when the victory is won, may I reach "heaven's joys, bright heaven's sun!" I don't understand heaven either, but if to be in heaven is to abide in God's presence, then I ask God to hold a place for me there. A lowly place will be sufficient. God will surely invite those countless (to me) sufferers now languishing in the dungeons and dung heaps of the earth to take the seats of honor at the heavenly banquet. I will be pleased to serve them at God's behest. To gaze upon God from the back of the room and wash the dishes after the guests have departed will be joy enough for me.

## PRAYER

Be thou my vision, O Lord of my heart, that knowing you intimately, I may love you deeply. My field of vision is full of so many other little things that I often miss you—or seeing you, I look past you. But more than that, when I look at those other little things, grant that I may see them as you see them. I often dismiss little things, including some people, brushing past them as if they were annoyances, distractions from the great business I have undertaken. But nothing, and certainly not your people whom I'm inclined to overlook, is an annoyance or distraction to you. Even the birds of the air are known to you; even the hairs of our heads are numbered by you.

What you disclose to me in your Christ, O Lord of my heart, is that I am your own, your beloved child, that you are ever with me and within me, "thou in me dwelling, and I one with thee." Shield me from the darts of the enemy, and when doubts and distractions intrude, do not let them define me. You define me, O Ruler of all. My ignorance notwithstanding, I am yours and you are mine.

*Amen.*

# 7

# COME DOWN, O LOVE DIVINE

Bianco da Siena (d. 1434)  Suggested tune: *Down Ampney*
tr. Richard Frederick Littledale (1833-1890)

*Come down, O love divine,*
*seek thou this soul of mine,*
*and visit it with thine own ardor glowing.*
*O Comforter, draw near,*
*within my heart appear,*
*and kindle it, thy holy flame bestowing.*

*O let it freely burn,*
*till earthly passions turn*
*to dust and ashes in its heat consuming;*
*and let thy glorious light*
*shine ever on my sight,*
*and clothe me round, the while my path illuming.*

*Let holy charity*
*mine outward vesture be,*
*and lowliness become mine inner clothing:*
*True lowliness of heart,*
*which takes the humbler part,*
*and o'er its own shortcomings weeps with loathing.*

*And so the yearning strong,*
*with which the soul will long,*
*shall far outpass the power of human telling,*
*for none can guess its grace,*
*till he become the place*
*wherein the Holy Spirit makes a dwelling.*

This hymn invites the Holy Spirit into the singer's heart. The rapturous, almost erotic imagery of the Latin original, by the Italian mystic Bianco da Siena, is typical of much medieval devotion and has been only slightly toned down in this Victorian-era translation. English composer Ralph Vaughan Williams wrote *Down Ampney* for this text. Down Ampney is the Cotswold village where Williams was born and raised and where his father was church organist. The tune was published in 1906.

*Come down, O love divine,*
    *seek thou this soul of mine,*
*and visit it with thine own ardor glowing.*
    *O Comforter, draw near,*
    *within my heart appear,*
*and kindle it, thy holy flame bestowing.*

So long have I been seeking you, O love divine, but I did not know it was you I sought. I hadn't known what or whom I sought, only that there was within me an empty place that cried out to be filled. I filled it, but with what did not satisfy, with the wrong things because I was looking in the wrong places, at the wrong times, and in the wrong company. Only you can fill the empty space within me, O love divine. And since I seem unable to find you, I shall stop trying to find you. I shall be still so that you can find me. "Seek thou this soul of mine."

I have known ardor but rarely your ardor. My ardor has come from the satisfaction of achieving my goals, but they were not always your goals and when achieved, they still left that empty place within me. Seek my soul, O love divine, "with thine own ardor glowing." Glow within me, and then shine out from me until all other glowings are subsumed in your light.

*O let it freely burn,*
*till earthly passions turn*
*to dust and ashes in its heat consuming;*
*and let thy glorious light*
*shine ever on my sight,*
*and clothe me round, the while my path illuming.*

You know, O love divine, how enamored I am of my earthly passions. Is it really necessary to burn them to dust and ashes? That seems extreme. Are my earthly passions such that they must be completely eradicated? Must you turn them all to dust and ashes? Do they *all* hold me back from receiving you? Is *every one* of them evil? Desirous as I am to receive you, I'm not sure about destroying my earthly passions. They are part of your creation, so how can they be bad? Surely you can leave me some bit of the pleasure I take from them.

And what if I change my mind? I may ask that you depart from me as your flame grows hot within me. If I change my mind, O love divine, then subdue me until I am forced to submit to you. And shine, glorious light, within and without, to my left and my right, above and below, before and behind, until I am luminous with your radiance.

*Let holy charity*
*mine outward vesture be,*
*and lowliness become mine inner clothing:*
*true lowliness of heart,*
*which takes the humbler part,*
*and o'er its own shortcomings weeps with loathing.*

Clothe me, O love divine, with a holy charity like yours, until
people see in me a lowliness of heart like yours. The heart
"which takes the humbler part" knows that this world is but
a speck of sand on the seashore. And when it comes to moral
character, I fall short of the mark and often can't even see
the mark.

Of what, then, can I boast? Give me a heart so lowly that
I make no distinctions among people. Any distinctions I
make would be based on partial evidence, for I cannot know
another's heart or what trials another has experienced. Had
I been subjected to the same, I might be less deserving than
those I presume to judge. If distinctions must be made,
you, O love divine, must make them. I suspect that the
distinctions you make will not be between the deserving
and undeserving but between the needy and those in a
position to give. Moved by holy charity, it is sufficient for
me that someone is in need. If that someone is undeserving,
may I open myself to her all the more, for it is among the
undeserving that a lowly and charitable heart can give its
greatest gift.

> And so the yearning strong,
>     with which the soul will long,
> shall far outpass the power of human telling,
>     for none can guess its grace,
>     till he become the place
> wherein the Holy Spirit makes a dwelling.

I've had enough of human telling. I've read all the books and
heard all the lectures. I've even written some of the books and
delivered some of the lectures. It's all worthless verbiage if it
does not open my heart to receive you, O love divine. So often

this verbiage has not opened my heart and I have not received you, receiving instead only the satisfaction that comes with scholarship and the praise of those who have heard and read my words. And so the yearning for you remains unabated, far outpassing the power of human telling. I give up on the noise of human telling, especially my own telling, in favor of silence and listening and waiting for you.

 **PRAYER**

Until you take up residence in my soul, O love divine, and begin to work your will in me, I cannot guess or imagine your grace because grace is just another word—a theological concept drawn from books and sermons, like a flavor known from a recipe card but never tasted. So Comforter, strengthener, wind and fire of God, blow through my heart, kindle and fan the flame you there have sparked into a blaze that consumes all within me that is not of you. Burn me, refine me, recreate me, possess me, ravish me, fill me.

*Amen.*

# 8

## COME, LABOR ON

Jane Laurie Borthwick (1813-1897)          Suggested tune: *Ora Labora*

*Come, labor on!*
*Who dares stand idle on the harvest plain,*
*while all around us waves the golden grain?*
*And to each servant does the Master say,*
*"Go, work today."*

*Come, labor on!*
*The enemy is watching night and day,*
*to sow the tares, to snatch the seed away;*
*while we in sleep our duty have forgot,*
*he slumbered not.*

*Come, labor on!*
*Away with gloomy doubts and faithless fear!*
*No arm so weak but may do service here:*
*by feeblest agents may our God fulfill*
*his righteous will.*

*Come, labor on!*
*Claim the high calling angels cannot share—*
*to young and old the gospel gladness bear:*
*redeem the time; its hours too swiftly fly.*
*The night draws nigh.*

*Come, labor on!*
*No time for rest, till glows the western sky,*
*till the long shadows o'er our pathway lie,*
*and a glad sound comes with the setting sun,*
*"Servants, well done."*

Jane Laurie Borthwick translated hymns from German into English and wrote several hymns of her own, of which this is the best known. She was a strong supporter of foreign missions and work among the homeless of Edinburgh. T. Tertius Noble, founder of the choir school at St. Thomas' Church in New York, wrote *Ora Labora* for this text. The text's optimistic outlook and the tune's dignified power made it an immediate favorite when it appeared for the first time in the Episcopal hymnal of 1916.

*Come, labor on!*
*Who dares stand idle on the harvest plain,*
*while all around us waves the golden grain?*
*And to each servant does the Master say,*
*"Go, work today."*

Idleness has its place. Some people are workaholics, driven by insecurity to succeed, earn respect, and prove themselves. Assuming too much responsibility, they often become burned out, angry, and withdrawn. They look right through you when talking to you. They need to stop, put their engines in idle, and do nothing for a while. This hymn is not for those people.

Other people have the opposite problem. I have worked with lazy colleagues. They rarely showed up on time and were often absent and unaccounted for. Some of them were charming, and some did good work—when they worked. But that wasn't often. They needed to shift into a higher gear and get the job done. This hymn is for them.

Spiritually healthy people strike a balance between working and idling. Secure in the knowledge of who they are, they know what they can do and what they can't do. They do what they can and either let others do the rest or leave the rest undone.

> Come, labor on!
> The enemy is watching night and day,
> to sow the tares, to snatch the seed away;
> while we in sleep our duty have forgot,
> he slumbered not.

The second stanza of this hymn is based on the parable of the weeds among the wheat in Matthew 13:24-30. After sowing seed, a farmer and his servants drifted off to sleep. While they slept, an enemy sowed weeds in the field alongside the wheat. When the shoots emerged from the ground and the servants noticed the weeds among the wheat, they offered to pull up the weeds. The farmer said no, lest they uproot the wheat along with the weeds. The farmer would divide the wheat from the weeds at harvest time.

Rest is necessary, both for its own sake and as preparation for work to be done later, but when the farmer dozes off, the enemy gains an opportunity to sow weeds. Our spiritual enemy never dozes. Even as we rest, let us be vigilant, not forgetting the work to which God calls us. And if the enemy is at work during our rest, may we know when we awake how to manage what the enemy has done. Sometimes the best course is simply to wait.

*Come, labor on!*
*Away with gloomy doubts and faithless fear!*
*No arm so weak but may do service here:*
*by feeblest agents may our God fulfill*
*his righteous will.*

"Gloomy doubts and faithless fear" are not uncommon among the servants of the Lord, but "no arm so weak but may do service here." God fulfills his righteous will by the feeblest of agents, even people troubled by gloomy doubts and faithless fear. I expect we're all feeble agents, even those of us who don't know we are. We might become stronger agents for God if we acknowledged our feebleness and dependence. For reasons known only to God, he seems to prefer working through such agents, and it's sometimes the feeblest agents whose witness shines most brightly.

*Come, labor on!*
*Claim the high calling angels cannot share—*
*to young and old the gospel gladness bear:*
*redeem the time; its hours too swiftly fly.*
*The night draws nigh.*

Angels are presumably a higher order of creation than human beings, but when God chose to enter his creation and bridge the gap between himself and his creation, he did not choose to become an angel but became one of us. In Jesus Christ God enfolded our humanity into himself. The Orthodox call this the deification of humanity. There are no mere humans, for God has fully and irrevocably united himself to us. The conviction that God did this is the only distinctive thing about Christian faith; it is what distinguishes Christianity from every other faith tradition in the world.

Hence, we have a "high calling angels cannot share." We alone (so far as we know) have experienced the grace of God on our own turf, on our own terms. We alone have that marvelous story to tell. God calls us to tell it to one another, of course, but perhaps also to the entire creation, including angels and whatever other orders of being God has seen fit to create.

> *Come, labor on!*
> *No time for rest, till glows the western sky,*
> *till the long shadows o'er our pathway lie,*
> *and a glad sound comes with the setting sun,*
> *"Servants, well done."*

A theological professor of mine didn't like this hymn because he considered it Pelagian. Pelagius was a fourth-century monk who carried on a spirited theological debate with Saint Augustine. The debate was over grace versus works. Augustine said that apart from grace, the power of God to transform human lives, no one can be in right relation with God; it is God and God alone who overcomes sin and evil. Pelagius, however, allowed for a role (albeit a limited one) for human free will. Augustine eventually prevailed, and Pelagius became one of the Christian church's most renowned heretics.

No doubt the words "Servants, well done" alarmed my professor. These words don't alarm me (though I am very fond of Augustine). Augustine powerfully probed the experience of grace transforming a human life when one's own efforts at reform fall short of the mark. I have experienced that, but I am not an inert object; God did not transform me the way a sculptor transforms stone. I had to say yes to God, and I could have said no.

The prospect of the words "Servant, well done," spoken by God at the end of my life, encourages me as I move haltingly along the road of faithful living. I hope to be a good servant of my Lord, not because I am strong or smart or courageous or virtuous, but because I have said yes to God who loves me and knows how to employ for his purposes even the feeblest agents.

## PRAYER

I don't want to stand idle, O God, but I don't know what to do. I've never known what to do. Sure, I have a good theological education, and I can make speeches and write books. But none of that amounts to much. When the chips are down, the right words rarely come to me.

Of course there's more to bringing in the harvest than words. Let me claim the high calling that angels cannot share. Send me again, O God, into the harvest and then work through me and my inadequacies to bring sight to the blind, make the lame walk, cleanse the lepers, give hearing to the deaf, raise the dead, and bring good news to the poor. I've tried to do that—sometimes—but send me out again. Here am I, send me! An obscure corner of the field will do. I so want to please you, to bring a smile to your face!

*"What makes you think you haven't already brought a smile to my face? If I had wanted you flawless, I'd have made you flawless. Go back into the harvest and see what you can do in the time remaining. Redeem the time. Don't worry about results. The shadows are lengthening, and soon I'll be calling you out of the harvest for good. And, don't waste time worrying about what you'll hear me say when you finally arrive home."*

*Amen.*

# 9

# COME, THOU FOUNT
# OF EVERY BLESSING

Robert Robinson (1735-1790)                    Suggested tune: *Nettleton*

*Come, thou fount of every blessing, tune my heart to sing thy grace!*
*Streams of mercy, never ceasing, call for songs of loudest praise.*
*Teach me some melodious sonnet, sung by flaming tongues above.*
*Praise the mount, O fix me on it, mount of God's unchanging love.*

*Here I find my greatest treasure; hither by thy help I've come;*
*and I hope, by thy good pleasure, safely to arrive at home.*
*Jesus sought me when a stranger, wandering from the fold of God.*
*He to rescue me from danger, interposed his precious blood.*

*Oh, to grace how great a debtor daily I'm constrained to be!*
*Let thy goodness, like a fetter, bind my wandering heart to thee.*
*Prone to wander, Lord, I feel it, prone to leave the God I love,*
*here's my heart, O take and seal it, seal it for thy courts above.*

When the dissolute young Robert Robinson attended a
meeting led by the famous Methodist evangelist George
Whitefield, he intended to scoff. But Robinson was so moved
that he was converted and eventually entered the Methodist
ministry. He later left Methodism to pastor an Independent

congregation, and then a Baptist congregation. Late in life, he was drawn to Unitarianism. This hymn was written in 1758 soon after his conversion to Methodism. The text has been significantly modified but retains the joyous, thankful tone of Robinson's original. *Nettleton* comes from the American folk tradition and has been published with various harmonies, meters, and time signatures.

*Come, thou fount of every blessing, tune my heart to sing thy grace!*
*Streams of mercy, never ceasing, call for songs of loudest praise.*
*Teach me some melodious sonnet, sung by flaming tongues above.*
*Praise the mount, O fix me on it, mount of God's unchanging love.*

This was my favorite hymn as a child. Perhaps it was the lilting tune *Nettleton* that appealed to me, but I suspect the hymn's buoyant text also spoke to me. From my earliest childhood until now, singing has always been my favorite part of church, and this hymn is about singing: "Tune my heart to sing thy grace! Teach me some melodious sonnet." The opening stanza asks that God, the "fount of every blessing," tune our hearts to sing of "streams of mercy, never ceasing," then suggests that these songs are also sung in heaven. The streams of divine mercy are not limited to the world we know.

*Here I find my greatest treasure; hither by thy help I've come;*
*and I hope, by thy good pleasure, safely to arrive at home.*
*Jesus sought me when a stranger, wandering from the fold of God.*
*He to rescue me from danger, interposed his precious blood.*

Some people think of the afterlife as their "greatest treasure," but this hymn suggests it is something immediate: "Here I find my greatest treasure." The "here" would be where we are right now, in this world, among our family and colleagues, with all the rough edges, bungled plans, and strained relationships that accompany this life. This should not surprise us, for it was into this world that God was born, lived, and died. God sought us and found us here, not in the by-and-by.

This stanza brings to mind the parable of the lost sheep in Luke 15. Jesus tells of a shepherd with responsibility for a hundred sheep. One of them wanders off and is lost. The shepherd leaves the ninety-nine unattended—a radical, and some would say, irresponsible thing to do—in search of the one sheep that is lost. God is wildly, extravagantly, irrationally generous in his care of us. If the sheep has strayed to the edge of a ravine, the shepherd will risk his life to rescue it, and when he finds it, he returns rejoicing. Countless stained-glass windows depict this scene, with the lost sheep lovingly draped around the shepherd's shoulders. Jesus identifies himself as that Good Shepherd in John 10. He seeks us out and rescues us right here, right now, in this life.

> Oh, to grace how great a debtor daily I'm constrained to be!
> Let thy goodness, like a fetter, bind my wandering heart to thee.
> Prone to wander, Lord, I feel it, prone to leave the God I love,
> here's my heart, O take and seal it, seal it for thy courts above.

Grace, God's undeserved goodness to us, surrounds us moment by moment. Every day our debt to divine grace grows greater, but it is a debt that we carry lightly, a debt that does not burden us because we know it will never be called in. Grace is a gift, not a loan to be repaid. It carries no I.O.U. and could not be repaid if it did. We receive God's grace with joy and thanksgiving, with no thought of payback.

The hymn's confident, joyous tone carries through to the end. Having celebrated God's grace in this life, it concludes with a prayer that God take and seal the singer's heart "for thy courts above."

## PRAYER

Let my prayer, Lord, be that of the early twentieth-century
Irish missionary Amy Carmichael:

> *Tune thou my harp;*
> *There is not, Lord, could never be,*
> *The skill in me.*

> *Tune thou my harp;*
> *That it may play thy melody,*
> *Thy harmony.*

> *Tune thou my harp;*
> *O Spirit, breathe thy thought through me,*
> *As pleaseth thee.*

Chain my heart to you, O God; handcuff it to you so that
it cannot wander. I know that love cannot be compelled,
so make the fetter binding my heart to you not something
external to myself, something I could resist, but the very state
of my heart itself. So enliven my heart and fill it with yourself
that wandering from you will be impossible because I cannot
conceive it.

Finally, when I come to the end of life, seal my heart, Lord,
for thy courts above. You have bestowed your bountiful grace
upon me here in this life. Make this life the antechamber to a
greater life to come, filled with grace upon grace.

*Amen.*

# 10

## FAIREST LORD JESUS

Anonymous, seventeenth century          Suggested tunes: *St. Elizabeth,*
*Schönster Herr Jesu*

Fairest Lord Jesus, Ruler of all nature,
O thou of God and man the Son,
thee will I cherish, thee will I honor,
thou, my soul's glory, joy, and crown.

Fair are the meadows, fairer still the woodlands,
robed in the blooming garb of spring:
Jesus is fairer, Jesus is purer,
who makes the woeful heart to sing.

Fair is the sunshine, fairer still the moonlight,
and all the twinkling starry host:
Jesus shines brighter, Jesus shines purer
than all the angels heaven can boast.

Beautiful Savior! Lord of all the nations!
Son of God and Son of Man!
Glory and honor, praise, adoration,
now and forever more be thine.

Both the German author and the English translator of this seventeenth-century hymn are anonymous. The tune *St. Elizabeth*, to which this text is most often sung, is of nineteenth-century Silesian origin and suggests warmth and tenderness. *Schönster Herr Jesu*, a seventeenth-century German melody, suggests depth and strength.

*Fairest Lord Jesus, Ruler of all nature,*
*O thou of God and man the Son,*
*thee will I cherish, thee will I honor,*
*thou, my soul's glory, joy, and crown.*

We have here a love song. Love songs don't deal in objective, verifiable facts. Someone in love expresses sentiments specific to a particular relationship. The superlative language used is not a negative comment on other relationships or other people. It is meaningful only within the context of that one relationship and would sound excessive or outlandish in another context. This hymn, this love song, is sung by someone in love with Jesus.

As the singer's beloved, Jesus is the one and only, above all others, the most beautiful, most delightful, most delectable, the fairest of all. This hymn is more about what's in the singer's heart than it is about Jesus, and as an expression of love, it's about both passion and commitment. As in a human marriage or friendship, commitment is the more important of the two. Passion is more exciting than commitment but less challenging. Passion comes and goes, is quickly aroused and quickly fades. Commitment is deeper. It is unaffected by changing circumstances and moods. Real love abides because it includes commitment.

We vow always to cherish and honor Jesus, much as a bride and groom pledge fidelity to one another. In a human marriage, misunderstandings, hurts, and betrayals occur, but the couple's love transcends such failures; forgiveness is given and accepted. We know that we will betray Jesus, but that Jesus will not betray us; Jesus will be faithful. That is why we can sing of Jesus as "my soul's glory, joy, and crown."

*Fair are the meadows, fairer still the woodlands,*
*robed in the blooming garb of spring:*
*Jesus is fairer, Jesus is purer,*
*who makes the woeful heart to sing.*

Many people marvel at natural beauty—mountain vistas, deep red sunsets, coral reefs, towering redwoods, colorful maples, and oaks draped in Spanish moss. Much of this book was written on my porch where I am surrounded by magnolias and pines and listen to a creek running nearby and the chorus of birds greeting the new day. The preponderance of evergreens makes "the blooming garb of spring" less dramatic in the Deep South than elsewhere, but even here a lush curtain of bright green suddenly swathes the subdued foliage of winter, and the first spring sunshine on my cheek indeed "makes the woeful heart to sing." To someone in love, the beloved is fairer than the fairest nature can offer.

But nature has its darker face, too. One animal survives by eating another. Storms, earthquakes, floods, and droughts devastate entire regions. Viruses and cancers claim human lives before their time. I don't give thanks for those things, and they certainly don't remind me how fair and pure Jesus is. Yet if Jesus is "Ruler of all nature," he reigns over nature's violence as well as its beauty, and if Jesus is good, then all of nature is good, even when it brings pain and loss. And of course Jesus, having himself experienced pain and loss, expresses more than a distant, academic sympathy to his grieving creatures. He embraces us and walks through the valley alongside us. That is perhaps the fairest, purest thing about him.

> *Fair is the sunshine, fairer still the moonlight,*
> *and all the twinkling starry host:*
> *Jesus shines brighter, Jesus shines purer*
> *than all the angels heaven can boast.*

The sun warming my cheek on a spring day is a delight, and the moonlight and starry host are indeed pleasing, but fair isn't the first word that comes to mind when I think of the heavens. The first word that occurs to me is incomprehensible. Astronomers and physicists have learned something about what we see in the sky, but every new discovery suggests a dozen perplexing new questions: Relativity. Quantum mechanics. The Big Bang. Black holes. String theory. Wave-particle duality. Dark matter. The Higgs boson. Gravity waves. Space and time warps. A hundred billion stars in our galaxy and another two trillion or so galaxies beyond our own—that's 250 galaxies for every person living today, containing more stars than there are grains of sand on earth. Some physicists even speculate about multiple universes. A gnat understands more of Shakespeare than we understand of what surrounds us on every side.

And yet the author of all this has sought us out. J.B. Phillips once referred to Earth as "the Visited Planet." Our little planet doesn't stand out among the celestial bodies; it doesn't even stand out in our own solar system. Its beauties—the meadows, the woodlands, the blooming garb of spring—are probably not unique in the universe and may be exceeded by beauties elsewhere. But ours is the planet and we are the creatures that the Maker of all things has visited in person. His visit to us is the brightest, purest, and fairest thing we know.

> *Beautiful Savior! Lord of all the nations!*
> *Son of God and Son of Man!*
> *Glory and honor, praise, adoration,*
> *now and forever more be thine.*

Beautiful is a word that doesn't often come to mind when I think of Jesus. It seems almost too trivial, too superficial, like something from an ad for cosmetics or lingerie. But that is outer beauty, something many people obsess about but which, even if attained, amounts to nothing. There is also an inner beauty that brightens everyone in its presence. Nowhere does it shine more brightly than from the heart of our "beautiful Savior." But of course beauty is in the eye of the beholder and those who focus their vision elsewhere will miss our beautiful Savior. He compels no one to see. You must stop and look.

## PRAYER

Beautiful Savior! You endow the universe with hints and traces of yourself. From the vastness of space to the infinitesimal smallness of subatomic particles, all things are beautiful because they flow from you and reflect you as a mirror reflects the sunlight. When I marvel at the splendors of nature, I see something of you in them. May I never fail to glorify, honor, praise, and adore you.

How would you have me express my adoration, beautiful Savior? I have no beauty of my own to offer. My thoughts, my relationships, my writings, my behavior, my worship, all that I am and ever will be—if any offering of mine is beautiful, it is because you make it so. All beauty is your beauty. Teach me to adore you, beautiful Savior, as you wish to be adored. Make me your beautiful servant.

Thank you for the pleasure I take in singing the hymns discussed in these pages. They are beautiful because of your presence in the hearts of their authors and composers. When I sing them, I intend them to express my adoration and submission to you as well. But a beautiful life is better than beautiful words. So fill my mind, my imagination, my heart, and my will, beautiful Savior, that every word that passes my lips may express the beauty of yourself dwelling within me. And then fill the minds, imaginations, hearts, and wills of all your creatures throughout the universe, those known to me and those unimaginable to me, that every word everywhere may be beautiful as you are beautiful.

*Amen.*

# 11

# FOR ALL THE SAINTS

William Walsham How (1823-1897)          Suggested tune: *Sine Nomine*

*For all the saints, who from their labors rest,*
*who thee by faith before the world confessed,*
*thy Name, O Jesus, be forever blessed.*
*Alleluia! Alleluia!*

*Thou wast their rock, their fortress, and their might;*
*thou, Lord, their captain in the well-fought fight;*
*thou, in the darkness drear, their one true light.*
*Alleluia! Alleluia!*

*O may thy soldiers, faithful, true, and bold,*
*fight as the saints who nobly fought of old,*
*and win with them the victor's crown of gold.*
*Alleluia! Alleluia!*

*O blest communion, fellowship divine!*
*we feebly struggle, they in glory shine;*
*yet all are one in thee, for all are thine.*
*Alleluia! Alleluia!*

*And when the strife is fierce, the warfare long,*
*steals on the ear the distant triumph song,*
*and hearts are brave again, and arms are strong.*
*Alleluia! Alleluia!*

*The golden evening brightens in the west;*
*soon, soon to faithful warriors comes their rest;*
*sweet is the calm of paradise the blessed.*
*Alleluia! Alleluia!*

*But lo! There breaks a yet more glorious day;*
*the saints triumphant rise in bright array;*
*the King of glory passes on his way.*
*Alleluia! Alleluia!*

*From earth's wide bounds, from ocean's farthest coast,*
*through gates of pearl streams in the countless host,*
*singing to Father, Son, and Holy Ghost:*
*Alleluia! Alleluia!*

William Walsham How was the first bishop of Wakefield in England. This is one of several of his hymns sung in churches today, but it had largely fallen out of use until Ralph Vaughan Williams composed *Sine Nomine* explicitly for this text. *Sine Nomine* means nameless. Vaughan Williams chose that name for his stirring tune because the names of most of the saints celebrated in this text are lost to history. Set to *Sine Nomine*, "For all the saints" has had a second life. Its popularity continues, and it is rarely sung today to any other tune.

*For all the saints, who from their labors rest,*
*who thee by faith before the world confessed,*
*thy Name, O Jesus, be forever blessed.*
*Alleluia! Alleluia!*

The word saint derives from the Latin *sanctus*, translating the Hebrew *kodesh*, meaning holy or set apart. To be a saint is to have been set apart in baptism. Every baptized person, every Christian, has been set apart for the glory of God.

Among all the saints, of course, are the great ones—the apostles, evangelists, and martyrs for whom churches are named and days are set aside in the church calendar. I need not list their names; you can read about them in the history books and on the internet.

But history has not looked kindly on some of the saints: medieval crusaders sacking Constantinople, Spanish inquisitors torturing Protestants and Jews, seventeenth and eighteenth-century slave traders, New England Puritans burning dissidents as witches, Southern Klansmen lynching innocent black men. Their faith was flawed, their witness misdirected, their legacy horrid. Yet they too were baptized and claimed the name of Christ; they too are numbered among all the saints.

Do we really want to celebrate *all* the saints? We certainly do. No Christian perfectly reflects the mind of our Lord, and the difference between the great saints and those we would never honor is merely one of degree. Moreover, we cannot know how history will judge us. Some of the causes we loudly promote in Jesus' name may not look so godly to future generations. The name of Jesus will "be forever blessed" because Jesus embraces all who seek to serve him, even those who do in his name things he would never have done. Perhaps he even embraces those who, for reasons unknown to us, curse his name.

*Thou wast their rock, their fortress, and their might;*
*thou, Lord, their captain in the well-fought fight;*
*thou, in the darkness drear, their one true light.*
*Alleluia! Alleluia!*

Most Christians like thinking of Christ as a rock, a fortress, strong. We long to stand on Christ the solid rock. But a rock is also hard. I prefer a Lord who is strong but who also shows a softer side.

Soldiers are to obey their captain, but we Christians often wander off and do as we please, paying mere lip service to our captain. The fight is not always "well fought." Many of us deserve to be court-martialed. But Christ doesn't do that. Is that the softer side of Christ the rock?

Christ "the one true light" exposes things as they are, not as we pretend they are. We see other people as they are—all their flaws and all their beauty. The true light also reveals us as we are—all hearts open, all desires known, no secrets hid. No more pretending. Some changes may be required.

*O may thy soldiers, faithful, true, and bold,*
*fight as the saints who nobly fought of old,*
*and win with them the victor's crown of gold.*
*Alleluia! Alleluia!*

The saint as Christian soldier is a popular image. Taken literally, however, it usually produces unhappy results

because we readily envision ourselves as carrying the banner
of Christ while identifying some other person, group, or
country as the embodiment of evil. History has judged very
few wars as genuine conflicts between good and evil. Most
wars, even those sanctioned by religious leaders, are later
deemed destructive, fruitless, and driven by hubris.

Yet we would be unwise to reject the image of the Christian
soldier. Let us indeed seek to "fight as the saints who nobly
fought of old," but to do so, we must recognize where the
battle occurs. It doesn't take place on land, sea, or air, but
inside the souls of the saints. When in our hubris we mistake
our own ideas and wishes for the will of God, we may try to
force them upon others. We are "faithful, true, and bold"
when we examine our souls and reject whatever we find
there that is not surrendered to our captain. The first thing
required for that is humility. Humility is also the second and
third thing. It may be the only thing.

Then, finally, after laying aside all our grand illusions, our
heads will be suited for "the victor's crown of gold."

> *O blest communion, fellowship divine!*
> *we feebly struggle, they in glory shine;*
> *yet all are one in thee, for all are thine.*
> *Alleluia! Alleluia!*

It turns out that I am not the splendid person I once fancied
myself to be. Like many young people, I set out believing that
my personality, wisdom, and skill would carry me over any
hurdle. When that didn't turn out well, I decided to focus
on the things I can do and let others do everything else, and
if some things didn't get done at all, we would still carry on.

All of history until the year 1944 had unfolded without me and the rest of history will soon do the same. My mark—if I leave a mark at all—will not be a blazing signpost for all to see. "You are a mist that appears for a little while and then vanishes," the Epistle of James happily reminds us (4:14). Or as someone once said, thrust your hand into a bucket of water and pull it out: the hole remaining is how much you'll be missed after you've gone.

Surprisingly, that realization was positive and liberating for me: I became more relaxed and rested, and although I undertook fewer tasks, I performed those tasks better. And other people surfaced who were eager to do what I could never have done. Everyone seemed happier. Certainly I was.

I now see the church as a collection of feebly struggling saints, including those still in this life and those above who "in glory shine." None of us would amount to much without the others. We are one, upholding and supporting one another, picking up after one another. We retain our individual identities but who we are together is far more than the sum of who we are individually—like the organs of the body, stones in a mosaic, instruments in an orchestra, threads in a coat, vegetables in a chowder. "O blessed communion, fellowship divine!"

*And when the strife is fierce, the warfare long,*
*steals on the ear the distant triumph song,*
*and hearts are brave again, and arms are strong.*
*Alleluia! Alleluia!*

"The strife is fierce, the warfare long" because we want to have it both ways. We want to be in right relationship with God, but we don't like what that requires. We would surrender our wills to God but with conditions and riders attached. We want to be faithful, but just on Sundays and perhaps alternate Tuesdays and Thursdays, unless something else comes up. We want a little bit of God but not too much. When that doesn't work for us, we grow disheartened and angry.

But through it all there "steals on the ear the distant triumph song." Sometimes its strains are muffled and sometimes we aren't paying attention to it. But even then, above the roar of competing noises, we hear, perhaps faintly, the chorus of the redeemed, sung by those who have strived and fought before us and have already found their place at the banquet table of the King. They are still our colleagues and companions in the way, and the assurance that their prayers surround and buttress us is a tonic to dispel the disheartened, angry moods that occasionally afflict even the most glorious saint.

We only hear that distant triumph song when we pause to listen for it. We find our way by walking a new path—the path of listening, stillness, and waiting. Then we feel ourselves picked up and carried along by all the saints. Our hearts are "brave, again, and arms are strong."

*The golden evening brightens in the west;*
*soon, soon to faithful warriors comes their rest;*
*sweet is the calm of paradise the blessed.*
*Alleluia! Alleluia!*

Now well into old age, I can see more clearly the golden evening brightening in the west. Although I feel certain of fewer things, I am increasingly comfortable with my ignorance, and death frightens me less than it once did.

Our images of what awaits us beyond that western horizon are mostly drawn from the Book of Revelation, and they can seem surprisingly mundane, even garish, if taken literally: pearly gates, streets of gold, crowns, white robes, waving palm branches, endless daylight, and lots of singing. I know better than to take those images literally, but they suggest one thing of which I'm increasingly certain: We will not be lonely in paradise but part of the great company of the redeemed. Coronation imagery may be the best we can come up with to describe it.

The Bible also speaks of the next life as one of rest and calmness. That rest is surely not sluggishness or inertia but a continual growing into the likeness of Christ. I understand "the calm of paradise the blessed" as a harmony arising from a union of wills. Paradise is where God's will is done; it is like the calm of the tonic chord into which a long progression of notes is finally resolved. Everything is in its place and all is well. In this life, that calm is seldom realized (though I believe it can be), but as we grow older, we have more time to pause and look for it and are more likely to recognize hints and anticipations of it. The people—mostly older folks—who do this are among the happiest and most blessed people I know. Lord, make me one of them.

> But lo! There breaks a yet more glorious day;
> the saints triumphant rise in bright array;
> the King of glory passes on his way.
> Alleluia! Alleluia!

The "yet more glorious day" envisioned here—more glorious than any day in this life—is the day of resurrection when "the saints triumphant rise in bright array." Several New

Testament authors speak of this day. What they say about it, both the scene itself and the timing of it, dumbfounds me, and I have long since given up trying to get my mind around it. When that day comes (assuming it comes in time and space as we know it), I suppose our questions will be either answered or shown to have been the wrong questions.

The part of the scene as envisioned in this stanza that most appeals to me is the passing by of the King of glory. I picture myself, together with those I have loved in this life, the many saints from history whose lives and writings have inspired me here, and God knows how many others, standing on the curb awaiting the King. Prophets, apostles, and martyrs pass before us. Choirs in procession are singing Bach, Handel, and Mendelssohn (or perhaps something even better). A more glorious parade has never been seen. Then the Lord Christ himself appears. "Thousand, thousand saints attending swell the triumph of his train" (see Hymn #24). That train grows moment to moment as it draws in each risen saint. It embraces me and those I love. As it embraces others, I notice some faces among the saints that surprise me—the Lord's standards seem to diverge from those I would have insisted on, and that makes this a "yet more glorious day."

*From earth's wide bounds, from ocean's farthest coast,*
*through gates of pearl streams in the countless host,*
*singing to Father, Son, and Holy Ghost:*
*Alleluia! Alleluia!*

So at last "through gates of pearl streams in the countless host" of every race, nation, and creed. There's the mother who prayed for her rebellious child, and there's the child.

Here comes a group of peasants who toiled in the shadow of a great cathedral they never entered. Sailors who plied the waves to introduce the good news to distant shores. Monks in their habits singing the daily offices. The sick now made whole, along with the nurses, physicians, and aides attending them. The mentally and physically challenged. The abused, the neglected, the taken for granted. Crime victims, judges, and prisoners. Pilgrims who fled persecution—and their persecutors! The newborn and the dying. The homeless and the destitute. Poor and rich, old and young, unworthy and worthy, befuddled and clear-headed, obscure and renowned, fearful and brave, weak and strong, liberal and conservative. Grandparents, parents, children, and those who are alone— all who for twenty centuries have worshiped their Lord in hundreds of thousands of churches in every latitude and longitude and altitude of the earth.

"From earth's wide bounds" they come. Running, walking, skipping, on crutches, in wheelchairs, carried on stretchers, laughing, and singing, they come. Not one of the saints is forgotten; each is now remembered and called by name. All are welcomed into the train of the King. Listen to their voices rising in a mighty chorus, "singing to Father, Son, and Holy Ghost: Alleluia! Alleluia!"

## PRAYER

Lord, I'm coming. Make me to be numbered with your saints, and when I pass through those gates of pearl, may I not be surprised to see who else is there.

*Amen.*

# 12

# GOD OF GRACE AND GOD OF GLORY

Harry Emerson Fosdick (1878-1969)          Suggested tune: *Cwm Rhondda*

God of grace and God of glory, on thy people pour thy power.
Crown thine ancient church's story, bring her bud to glorious flower.
Grant us wisdom, grant us courage, for the facing of this hour.

Lo! the hosts of evil 'round us scorn thy Christ, assail his ways.
From the fears that long have bound us,
    free our hearts to faith and praise.
Grant us wisdom, grant us courage, for the living of these days.

Cure thy children's warring madness, bend our pride to thy control.
Shame our wanton selfish gladness, rich in things and poor in soul.
Grant us wisdom, grant us courage, lest we miss thy kingdom's goal.

Set our feet on lofty places, gird our lives that they may be
armored with all Christ-like graces; set, O God, thy people free.
Grant us wisdom, grant us courage, that we fail not man nor thee.

Save us from weak resignation to the evils we deplore.
Let the search for thy salvation be our glory evermore.
Grant us wisdom, grant us courage, serving thee whom we adore.

Written during the Great Depression and between the World Wars, this hymn is a plea for deliverance from the pride and fear that lead to war and injustice. Baptist clergyman and professor Harry Emerson Fosdick wrote the lyrics in 1930 for the dedication of the Riverside Church in New York, where he was pastor. *Cwm Rhondda* was composed in 1905 by Welsh composer John Hughes.

⸻ ❦ ⸻

*God of grace and God of glory, on thy people pour thy power.*
*Crown thine ancient church's story, bring her bud to glorious flower.*
*Grant us wisdom, grant us courage, for the facing of this hour.*

The "ancient church's story" is an uneven one. On the one hand are the great saints who inspire us to live a holy life. They prove that radical obedience is possible. The light of Christ shone out from them and brightened the world in their day. It brightens our world still.

But the church's story also includes cynical careerists, arrogant prelates who acted like all-powerful potentates, corrupt rulers who crushed the poor, and many rigid, self-righteous prigs. And then there are the untold millions of tawdry, petty, selfish, worldly people who, though baptized into Christ, displayed little sign of it. We can be glad that most of them have left no mark, but they, too, are part of the church's story. Bringing the church's story to "glorious flower" will take place only when all of us are willing to be empowered by the God of grace and glory.

*Lo! the hosts of evil 'round us scorn thy Christ, assail his ways.*
*From the fears that long have bound us,*
*   free our hearts to faith and praise.*
*Grant us wisdom, grant us courage, for the living of these days.*

"The hosts of evil 'round us" are always in the news, while
the hosts of evil within us are less often acknowledged. But
the evil outside flows from the evil within. It has ever been
so. Intentional, willful acts on our part "scorn thy Christ,
assail his ways." Natural disasters can be horrific, but they are
not willfully committed. The place to start combating evil is
within ourselves.

"The fears that long have bound us" bind us still. As I
write these words, millions of Middle Eastern Muslims and
Christians are seeking refuge elsewhere because war has
devastated their lives at home. But fear often overrules our
humane instincts and denies desperate people a generous
and compassionate welcome among us.

Although that situation is extreme, it is not unique. Fear has
always driven people to circle the wagons and shrink from
engaging other people. In 1939, the United States turned
away a ship from Germany with 937 mostly Jewish refugees
for fear that they might be Communists. The Nazis later
murdered most of them.

The more someone differs from us, the more fearful we
become. Assisting our neighbor next door is one thing,
but assisting someone from another country who speaks
a different language, has a different skin color, or follows
a different religion is something else. Add the threat of
terrorism, and fear often trumps every noble thought.

*Cure thy children's warring madness, bend our pride to thy control.*
*Shame our wanton selfish gladness, rich in things and poor in soul.*
*Grant us wisdom, grant us courage, lest we miss thy kingdom's goal.*

Most people love their country, and I certainly love mine. I celebrate all that is good about America. But no country is right all the time, and America's sins are magnified for all to see because of our economic and military prominence. Try as it might, the rest of the world cannot ignore us. That's why when we engage in "warring madness" or behave in proud or selfish ways, people take note. Our huge consumption of the world's resources and the entertainment, fashions, and armaments we export overseas also suggest to some that we are "rich in things and poor in soul."

*Set our feet on lofty places, gird our lives that they may be*
*armored with all Christ-like graces; set, O God, thy people free.*
*Grant us wisdom, grant us courage, that we fail not man nor thee.*

"Lofty places" are those from which we can see everything and see it accurately. Too often we lower our gaze and look only at what is close and familiar to us. Not seeing the larger world, we care only for those nearby. This narrow provincialism enslaves people and winks as others enslave them. We claim adherence to high principles and standards but act on them only when they benefit us and people like us.

*Save us from weak resignation to the evils we deplore.*
*Let the search for thy salvation be our glory evermore.*
*Grant us wisdom, grant us courage, serving thee whom we adore.*

Most of us deplore evil in the abstract. We dislike dictators. We disapprove of racism. We'd like to eliminate crime and corruption. We don't want people to starve. We favor freedom, justice, world peace, and equal opportunity for all. But the evils we deplore seem to thrive despite our disapproval, perhaps for lack of will on our part or because our political system is malfunctioning. So we retreat into our homes behind locked doors with climate control, mix a drink, and watch television, preferring shows that entertain rather than inform or challenge us. We hope someone— perhaps the next president?—will address these evils and set them right. But we don't count on it. We stop paying attention. Our souls grow numb.

Another word for resignation is indifference. Holocaust survivor Elie Wiesel wrote, "The opposite of love is not hate, it's indifference. The opposite of art is not ugliness, it's indifference. The opposite of faith is not heresy, it's indifference. And the opposite of life is not death, it's indifference."

Although few of us can reform the economic and political order, all of us can make a difference. In a well-known story, a boy, noticing that dozens of starfish were washing up on the shore and dying in the hot sun, picked one up and threw it back into the sea. "Saving one starfish won't make any difference," his father said. "It will make a big difference to that one," the boy replied.

## PRAYER

God of grace and God of glory, empower us to do and be what you would have us do and be. Make our church and our nation not only strong but holy, O God. Plant within us a sense of responsibility for one another, especially for the poor and powerless. Make us good stewards of this fragile earth, our island home. Along with our strength, give us humility—and if possible, give us humility without humiliation. Teach us moderation. Tame our pride. Open our eyes to see all people everywhere as your beloved children and our beloved brothers and sisters, created in your image, whom you love with an infinite love, and whom you sent your Son to redeem. Then give us a generous heart to share our abundance with them and to welcome those who come to our shores seeking a better life.

Set our feet on lofty places, O God, where we will be astonished by what we see. Pry open our minds to embrace your startling truth. Then give us courage to reorder our lives in its light. Inspire us to set your people free: free from fear, prejudice, neglect, violence, and abuse. Looking at us, Lord, may your people see the face of Christ.

*Amen.*

# 13

## GUIDE ME, O THOU GREAT JEHOVAH

William Williams (1717-1791)                    Suggested tune: *Cwm Rhondda*
tr. Peter Williams (1722-1796) and the author

*Guide me, O thou great Jehovah, pilgrim through this barren land;*
*I am weak, but thou art mighty; hold me with thy powerful hand;*
*bread of heaven, bread of heaven, feed me now and evermore.*

*Open now the crystal fountain, whence the healing stream doth flow;*
*let the fire and cloudy pillar lead me all my journey through;*
*strong deliverer, strong deliverer, be thou still my strength and shield.*

*When I tread the verge of Jordan, bid my anxious fears subside;*
*death of death, and hell's destruction, land me safe on Canaan's side;*
*songs of praises, songs of praises, I will ever sing to thee.*

Wales is known for a rich tradition of Christian hymnody, and
William Williams (1717-1791) is widely regarded as the greatest
in the long line of great Welsh hymnists. He wrote roughly
900 hymns, mostly in Welsh, the tongue in which Welsh
congregations still sing them today. This hymn is considered
Williams's most beloved. Peter Williams (no relation to the
author) translated the opening stanza into English; the
author himself translated the second and third stanzas. Welsh

regiments in World War I sang this hymn to keep their spirits up, and it is sung in Wales today on both sacred and secular occasions. The text has been set to over forty tunes. The robust *Cwm Rhondda*, composed in 1905 by Welsh composer John Hughes, is the one to which it is usually sung today. A better musical fit for the text is hard to imagine.

*Guide me, O thou great Jehovah, pilgrim through this barren land; I am weak, but thou art mighty; hold me with thy powerful hand; bread of heaven, bread of heaven, feed me now and evermore.*

This hymn recalls the story of the Israelites' forty years of desert wandering. The name Jehovah (a variant of the Hebrew divine name disclosed to Moses) and the references to the barren desert, bread from heaven, the crystal fountain and its healing stream, the fire and cloudy pillar, and the crossing of the Jordan into the land of Canaan (the Promised Land) all recall incidents in that seminal story.

But the hymn isn't really about that story. It's about a lost soul searching for solace and a safe landing; it is that lost soul's plea for deliverance. The tale of the Israelites' wandering becomes the story of every Christian (and I think Jews could sing this hymn as well) on a journey from faithlessness into faithfulness, from error into truth.

The land where my soul lives hardly seems barren. I enjoy many comforts and amenities. But the landscape within me sometimes feels like the desert through which the Israelites wandered for forty long years. A loving and just God may guide and feed me, but like the ancient Israelites, I often don't believe it and try to hedge my bets and cover my bases. I hold back from trusting God completely.

It's not that my intentions are bad but that my will is weak. My soul hungers for food that satisfies, yet I eat the food that pleases for the moment but builds no strength. It's as if my diet consisted exclusively of donuts: The taste is agreeable, but both body and mind grow lethargic. I become restless and unfocused. Then I wonder what's the matter.

Hence, I pray to God: "Hold me with thy powerful hand." I need to be held both to constrain me when I am unwilling to look beyond momentary pleasures and to guide me when I am willing. I ask for the nourishing bread of heaven that only God can provide.

> Open now the crystal fountain, whence the healing stream doth flow;
> let the fire and cloudy pillar lead me all my journey through;
> strong deliverer, strong deliverer, be thou still my strength and shield.

The "crystal fountain" refers to the water the Lord produced from a desert rock when the Israelites murmured and "tested the LORD, saying, 'Is the LORD among us or not?'" (Exodus 17:1-7) One might think that in asking for the crystal fountain to be opened now, we are behaving as those ancient Israelites did, but while I am not above murmuring and trying to test God, that's not where my heart is when I sing this hymn. Rather, I feel like the deer in Psalm 42: "As the deer longs for the water-brooks, so longs my soul for you, O God. My soul is athirst for God, athirst for the living God; when shall I come to appear before the presence of God?"

I don't hold God accountable when I find myself in a spiritual desert, but I often complain to God as if my desert were God's doing. I ask only that God come to me and deliver me. It is not so much the water as God himself that I long for.

*When I tread the verge of Jordan, bid my anxious fears subside;*
*death of death, and hell's destruction, land me safe on Canaan's side;*
*songs of praises, songs of praises, I will ever sing to thee.*

That longing for God will, I suspect, continue right up to my final day. I have no "anxious fears" about the punishment or torments of hell—that would be out of character for a loving God. The God disclosed in Jesus Christ seeks not to punish sinners but to change and redeem them. But what if there is no God? What if the universe is nothing more than a vast mechanical and chemical jumble with no purpose or direction? What makes me anxious is the possibility of nothingness after I die. That strikes me as an odd thing to fear, since if there is nothing, then there can be no disappointment or pain. But there would also be no one to love, no goals to strive for, no new discoveries to make. I would like to know that in some way, my identity, my self—transformed, I hope into a far better version of the person I am today—will survive the death of my body. The New Testament promises that, but I still wonder. That's what I have in mind when I sing, "Land me safe on Canaan's side."

## ⬥⬥⬥ **PRAYER** ⬥⬥⬥

The ancient Israelites promised to be faithful to you, great Jehovah, yet their commitment waxed hot and cold. They trusted you one minute and trusted themselves the next. Their faith flamed brightly, then flickered and cooled. I am one of those Israelites. Like them, I promise to trust and follow you, but then my commitment flickers and cools. I am faithful enough when passing through cheery meadowlands, but in the desert, I forget you. I grumble and complain. You can't count on me.

Yet as you did not forsake the Israelites long ago, great Jehovah, do not now forsake me. "Open now the crystal fountain," open it to me and send your "fire and cloudy pillar" to guide me! I promise, yet again, that I will trust and follow you. I have promised many times before but allow me to promise this one time more. And if I break my promise again, then allow me to promise again and again and again, until I have surrendered all that I am to you and no more promising is needed because the path of not trusting and following you will have vanished before me.

Someday, perhaps today, I shall arrive at "the verge of Jordan" and gaze across to the other side. Then, taking the step that everyone must take, I shall step into the river and cross over. What awaits me there, Lord? The Promised Land? Heaven? Paradise? So I've been taught, but how can I, who know so little even about this life, presume to know about the next life? Standing at the river's edge, I am afraid, O great Jehovah. I fear you will not know me when I arrive on the other side. I fear you will not be there at all, that no one will be there. I fear the other side will be a complete blank. But cross that river I shall.

As with everything, it comes down to two words: trust and follow. Jesus, you have stood on this shore, gazed across to the other side, and crossed this river before me. I need not fear because you have been here and you are the "death of death, and hell's destruction." When I step away from this shore and the water rises around me, hold me tight, blessed Jesus. Then "land me safe on Canaan's side," that there I may join my voice to those of the multitudes arrived before me—blessed souls who, like me, feared to tread the verge of Jordan but trusted and followed you. "Songs of praises, songs of praises," we will ever sing to thee.

*Amen.*

# 14

## HILLS OF THE NORTH, REJOICE

Charles Edward Oakley (1802-1880)

Suggested tunes:
Little Cornard, Darwall's 148th

Hills of the north, rejoice;
river and mountain-spring,
hark to the advent voice;
valley and lowland sing:
Though absent long, your Lord is nigh;
he judgment brings and victory.

Isles of the southern seas,
deep in your coral caves,
pent be each warring breeze,
lulled be your restless waves:
He comes to reign with boundless sway,
and makes your wastes his great highway.

Lands of the east, awake,
your people shall be free;
the sleep of ages break,
and rise to liberty.
On your far hills, long cold and gray,
has dawned the everlasting day.

Shores of the utmost west,
ye that have waited long,
unvisited, unblessed,
break forth to swelling song;

*high raise the note, that Jesus died,*
*yet lives and reigns, the Crucified.*

*Shout, while ye journey home;*
*songs be in every mouth;*
*lo, from the north we come,*
*from east and west and south.*
*City of God, the bond are free,*
*we come to live and reign in thee!*

This hymn speaks to both missionary and Advent themes. The strong, evocative imagery in Charles Edward Oakley's original text captures the sense of yearning for redemption felt by many Christians and others. Oakley was an attorney and priest of the Church of England. *Little Cornard* was written for this text by English composer and hymnal editor Martin Shaw, brother of Geoffrey Shaw. It was published in 1915. *Darwall's 148th*, by John Darwall, an English clergyman, was published in 1770.

*Hills of the north, rejoice;*
*river and mountain-spring,*
*hark to the advent voice;*
*valley and lowland sing:*
*Though absent long, your Lord is nigh;*
*he judgment brings and victory.*

We cannot move. We stand like bleak, paralyzed monoliths. It's as if frozen soil encases our feet, iron-like, lifeless. The rivers and seas are ice to the very bottom; nothing swims in them. There are no living sounds because there are no creatures to make the sounds. But we remember, vaguely, the stories from long ago, stories of other times and other places, when camellias fluttered in the breeze, birdsongs filled the air, otters played on the riverbanks, and the brooks ran freely to the sea.

A voice is singing "Rejoice!" But who could rejoice in this cold?

"Though absent long, your Lord is nigh." There was something about a Lord in the old stories, a Lord who healed the sick, stilled the sea, and raised the dead. But we stopped acting on the stories, then we stopped believing them, and then we stopped telling them, until now we hardly remember them. But some do remember, and now a voice cries that our Lord, though absent long, is near.

But is that good news? "He judgment brings and victory." Judgment on whom? Will he judge us? There was always judgment in the old stories. By what right does the Lord return to judge? We did not invite him. This is our ice, and we've accepted it. But the voice keeps singing.

> Isles of the southern seas,
> deep in your coral caves,
> pent be each warring breeze,
> lulled be your restless waves:
> He comes to reign with boundless sway,
> and makes your wastes his great highway.

The "warring breezes" are in fact wildly destructive storms and the "restless waves" giant tsunamis. There are the breezes and waves of selfishness. Everything is evaluated on the basis of economics. If it expands the economy, we bow before it and ask no questions. There are the breezes and waves of indifference. Are babies slaughtered? Does our government attack and destroy in our name? Are innocent people incarcerated and executed? Do the rich grow richer while the poor grow poorer? We don't want to hear about it. There are the breezes and waves of hubris. We tell ourselves: "We are right; they are wrong; we must compel them to become as we are. God wills it." Then we retreat into the company of the like-minded. Our prayers are not prayers of penitence.

Although we have accustomed ourselves to our warring breezes and restless waves, we don't like the wreckage they create. Won't someone recreate our world, contain our warring breezes, and still our restless waves? Could change be coming?

*Lands of the east, awake,*
*your people shall be free;*
*the sleep of ages break,*
*and rise to liberty.*
*On your far hills, long cold and gray,*
*has dawned the everlasting day.*

Too long have our souls been cold and gray. Too long have we wandered aimlessly. Dazed and numbed, we have refused to notice the important things. From time to time, it is true, we heard rumors and secondhand reports and might have inquired further had we not drifted with the winds. We have moved without going anywhere, listened without hearing, spoken without saying anything. We were there but not present. We have merely taken up space.

The hurt was too much. We were afraid. We didn't want to exhaust ourselves and so resigned ourselves to the familiar. We drifted here, there, anywhere. People were born, got married and divorced, moved from job to job and house to house, and then died. Empires rose and fell. But it never added up to much. It feels as if we're just waiting—waiting for the light to change, for bedtime, for next year, for Christ to return, for whatever. Isn't something else supposed to happen?

> Shores of the utmost west,
> ye that have waited long,
> unvisited, unblessed,
> break forth to swelling song;
> high raise the note, that Jesus died,
> yet lives and reigns, the Crucified.

"Unvisited, unblessed?" Unvisited by whom? Unblessed by whom? I'm beginning to remember the old stories now, stories about the Lord, about a visitation, a blessing. They said God had visited and blessed us. The Crucified and the King are the same, the stories said. They told of the One with bleeding hands and thorn-scarred brow who is Ruler of all things. He is here, has always been here, the stories said. If we have felt unvisited and unblessed, waiting for something else, is it because we did not see what was unfolding around us or open our hearts to invite him in? He dwells only where he is invited and where his reign is owned.

Wake up! Look! Pay attention! Over the far hills, long cold and gray, a glimmer appears. It's still gray but a lighter shade of gray. The air is churning, and birds are rustling. The sleep of ages is ending. From beyond the eastern sky, the King approaches!

> *Shout, while ye journey home;*
> *songs be in every mouth;*
> *lo, from the north we come,*
> *from east and west and south.*
> *City of God, the bond are free,*
> *we come to live and reign in thee!*

At last we come. From the north we come. The steely ice melts in the radiance of his face. How can we shrink from a Judge who suffers as he suffers, who loves as he loves? From the south we come. Our selfishness is transformed into selflessness, our indifference into compassion, our hubris into humility. From the east we come, awakened now to greet his dawn. He shines upon us and within us, brightening every shadow, enlightening every thought. From the west we come. Visited, blessed, no longer waiting, we place our hands in his, ready to live, ready to die, ready to rise and reign with him.

## ∞— PRAYER —∞

Come, Lord Jesus! Claim us for your own; form us once again into your image. Set us free from the bonds that bind us, and never mind that they have bound us because we chose them. A new thing is unfolding, something we did not, could not have imagined. Dayspring has arrived!

Come, Lord Jesus! We fling wide the doors of our hearts! We await you, knowing that you are already at the door, already entering in. Fill and possess us, Lord Jesus. May we never again want or wait for anything but you. You come to us, suffer for us, embrace us, and call us by name.

Now we also come to you, to accompany you on your journey home, our journey home. We shout as we make our way, songs on every tongue. We praise you, O God, we acknowledge you to be the Lord. Hands linked with apostles, prophets, martyrs, and myriads of saints, we bow and adore you. From north, south, east, and west we come, shouting, singing, dancing as we go. Make our hearts your throne, Lord Jesus, and then claim the crown for your own.

*Amen.*

# 15

## HOW FIRM A FOUNDATION

Anonymous, eighteenth century                    Suggested tunes: *Lyons, Foundation*

*How firm a foundation, ye saints of the Lord,*
*is laid for your faith in his excellent Word!*
*What more can he say than to you he hath said,*
*to you who for refuge to Jesus have fled?*

*"Fear not, I am with thee, O be not dismayed,*
*for I am thy God and will still give thee aid.*
*I'll strengthen thee, help thee, and cause thee to stand,*
*upheld by my righteous, omnipotent hand."*

*"When through the deep waters I call thee to go,*
*the rivers of woe shall not thee overflow;*
*for I will be with thee thy troubles to bless*
*and sanctify to thee thy deepest distress."*

*"When through fiery trials thy pathway shall lie,*
*my grace, all-sufficient, shall be thy supply.*
*The flames shall not hurt thee; I only design*
*thy dross to consume and thy gold to refine."*

*"The soul that on Jesus hath leaned for repose*
*I will not, I will not, desert to his foes.*
*That soul, though all hell should endeavor to shake,*
*I'll never, no never, no never, forsake."*

Published in 1787, this hymn is based on Isaiah 43:2-3: "When you pass through the waters, I will be with you; and through the rivers, they shall not overwhelm you; when you walk through fire you shall not be burned, and the flame shall not consume you. For I am the LORD your God, the Holy One of Israel, your Savior." The hymn's anonymous author applies these words to Jesus. *Lyons*, by William Gardiner (See Hymn #40), was published in 1815 and brings out the text's robust, sturdy elements, while *Foundation*, by an unknown composer and first appearing in 1835, can suggest a more tender interpretation.

*How firm a foundation, ye saints of the Lord,*
*is laid for your faith in his excellent Word!*
*What more can he say than to you he hath said,*
*to you who for refuge to Jesus have fled?*

Most people seek a solid foundation, and they try to build it themselves, through education, hard work, networking, personality, and marrying well. This often works for a while. They get a job, make connections, and gain a reputation. They are promoted and granted entry into select circles. But soon, often in middle age, the emptiness of a life built on such a foundation becomes clear. Careers level out. The big house no longer satisfies. People begin drinking too much. Marriages fray or dissolve. With singer Peggy Lee, people ask, "Is that all there is?" They fear the answer is yes.

Nations do the same. They seek security through the force of arms and draconian laws, clutching what they have and barring the door to migrants and refugees. National life begins to center around dominance rather than service, strength rather than justice, keeping rather than giving. Citizens of other nations (and some of their own citizens as well) feel estranged and excluded from the common life. The foundation starts to crumble. Things fall apart. Anger and finger-pointing ensue. The prophet Isaiah repeatedly warned ancient Judah against basing national life on such a foundation.

A better foundation is laid in the Word. This may refer either to Jesus Christ, the definitive communication of God to humanity, or to the Bible, the written record of that communication. Not many people and not many nations stand on that foundation. The few who do put ambition, willfulness, and selfishness aside and prosper in the only way that matters.

> *"Fear not, I am with thee, O be not dismayed,*
> *for I am thy God and will still give thee aid.*
> *I'll strengthen thee, help thee, and cause thee to stand,*
> *upheld by my righteous, omnipotent hand."*

*"What are you afraid of? What holds you back? Are you afraid you'll fail? I was crucified, and that meant I failed. You too will fail. Everyone fails. Don't be afraid of failure. Success teaches you nothing, but you learn and grow from your failures, and when you begin again after failing, you come back stronger and wiser. My failure redeemed the world.*

*"Are you afraid you'll lose something? I had nowhere to lay my head. Poverty forced upon someone is painful, but*

when poverty is a choice embraced with grace and humility,
it liberates you from the tyranny of things. Wealth is more
dangerous than poverty. Quit grasping. Don't be afraid to let
go of things.

"Are you afraid to be alone? I often went up to the mountain
to be alone. Loneliness can lead to self-pity, but being alone
can also give you solitude, the space to explore who you are and
to invite me to draw closer to you. Don't be afraid to be alone.

"Are you afraid to die? Some deaths are tragic and painful, but
death itself is part of life as my Father created it. It is the final
act of letting go, of surrender into the arms of God. Don't be
afraid to die. Only by dying can you experience resurrection.

"'Fear not, I am with thee.' You will experience pains,
sorrows, losses, difficulties, and disappointments, but 'I'll
strengthen thee, help thee, and cause thee to stand, upheld
by my righteous, omnipotent hand.' Do not be afraid."

> "When through the deep waters I call thee to go,
> the rivers of woe shall not thee overflow;
> for I will be with thee thy troubles to bless
> and sanctify to thee thy deepest distress."

"I have visited all your deepest and darkest places. My
hometown dismissed me as nothing. Then wherever I went,
people misunderstood and maligned me. I was homeless
and depended on the generosity of others. When ill, I lacked
medical care. One of my closest friends betrayed me and then
all my friends abandoned me. I was arrested on a trumped-
up charge, then convicted, mocked, humiliated, and killed.
I thought God had forsaken me. You talk about your deep

waters and rivers of woe. I know those places. I have claimed them, sanctified them, and made them my own. I am with you always, everywhere, but especially there.

"Are you tempted to give up? So was I. Does everything seem meaningless to you? It did to me, too. Do you see only darkness extending beyond the horizon in every direction? I know that darkness. Do you think that you lack the energy to take one more step? So did I.

"Don't give up. Take one more step, and then another, until a glimmer of light appears. Then move toward that glimmer. It will grow brighter until it finally becomes a luminous presence. I always took the next step. You can too, because I have been where you are. Let your rivers of woe turn you to me. 'I will be with thee thy troubles to bless, and sanctify to thee thy deepest distress.'"

> "When through fiery trials thy pathway shall lie,
> my grace, all-sufficient, shall be thy supply.
> The flames shall not hurt thee; I only design
> thy dross to consume and thy gold to refine."

"The flames need not hurt you. Consider the fire that burns inside you: the heat of anger, the smoldering coals of envy, the flames of passion. I was often angry, but I acted on anger only once, at those who transformed my Father's house into a shopping mall. I was then convicted of a crime I didn't commit, but if I had lashed out at my accusers, would it have achieved anything? As for envy, I lived simply, but I had enough, so why envy others? Don't you have enough? I was passionate with all the desires any young man feels, but they

*didn't control me. My inner life wasn't a fiery trial, and yours
need not be.*

*"Consider also the fire that burns outside you. Warplanes
bomb your neighborhood, terrorists blow up marketplaces
and airliners, diabolical gunmen shoot innocent people.
When other souls are scorched with hatred, the flames
sometimes burn the innocent. Those flames can hurt you
and you cannot quench them. Until all the world is gathered
into my arms, that's not going to change. When you are the
one burned and your heart breaks, I burn and weep with you.
Let me hold you in my arms.*

*"And remember that fiery trials can lead to nobility of character,
a wider sympathy for others, and a deeper commitment to
justice. Courageously borne, pain produces serenity. 'I only
design thy dross to consume, thy gold to refine.'"*

> "The soul that on Jesus hath leaned for repose
> I will not, I will not, desert to his foes.
> That soul, though all hell should endeavor to shake,
> I'll never, no never, no never, forsake."

*"Come to me and lean on me. I see you stumbling,
exhausted, confused, burdened by guilt and regrets. Let it go.
Let me carry your burden. My yoke is easy and my burden—
your burden—is light.*

*"Why do you hold back? Do you like where you are, what
you are? Perhaps it's that you know my repose is something
other than a perpetual nap. My repose is rest for the soul,
but it also includes doing, growing, becoming more than you*

are, more than you can even dream of. I offer serenity, not somnolence; solitude, but with companionship, fellowship, communion, engagement. There will be pain, but I will help you rise above the pain. I offer you myself.

"The powers of hell will 'endeavor to shake' you. They will sing sweet songs into your ear, hold delectable treats before you, tell you that you have been mistreated and tricked and deserve a better deal and more of whatever pleases you. The powers of hell know your weakest places. That's where they have gained entry into your soul in the past and they will try it again. They know you well and they do not give up easily.

"But I have defeated the powers of hell, and you are my beloved whom 'I'll never, no never, no never, forsake.'"

## PRAYER

I hear you, Lord Jesus, and I pray that I may lean on you for repose, but I also pray for others. The deep waters and fiery trials I've experienced, though stressful and dispiriting, have been negligible compared to those of so many others. I pray for refugees fleeing their war-torn homelands, the homeless on our city streets, spouses trapped in abusive marriages, victims of substance abuse, prisoners, the discouraged and depressed, and those dying destitute and alone. Many of them, I know, have never heard of you. Some are so exhausted trying to survive that they lack the leisure hours I enjoy to sing hymns and pray to you. I take comfort from your assurance, Lord Jesus, that you will "never, no never, no never, forsake" me, and I ask that you give that assurance to those others as well. And if I can be the means by which you give that assurance, guide me to give it in the spirit so that it may be received.

*Amen.*

# 16

## I BOW MY FOREHEAD TO THE DUST

John Greenleaf Whittier (1807-1892)          Suggested tune: *The Third Tune*

I bow my forehead to the dust, I veil mine eyes for shame,
and urge, in trembling self-distrust, a prayer without a claim.
No offering of my own I have, nor works my faith to prove;
I can but give the gifts God gave, and plead his love for love.

I dimly guess, from blessings known, of greater out of sight;
and, with the chastened psalmist, own God's judgments too are right.
And if my heart and flesh are weak to bear an untried pain,
the bruisèd reed God will not break, but strengthen and sustain.

I know not what the future hath of marvel or surprise,
assured alone that life and death God's mercy underlies.
And so beside the silent sea I wait the muffled oar:
no harm from God can come to me on ocean or on shore.

I know not where God's islands lift their fronded palms in air;
I only know I cannot drift beyond his love and care.
And thou, O Lord, by whom are seen thy creatures as they be,
forgive me if too close I lean my human heart on thee.

John Greenleaf Whittier was an American Quaker journalist, editor, and poet. Although he did not regard himself as a hymnist—because he said he knew almost nothing about music (and perhaps because Quaker worship rarely includes singing)—165 of his poems have been set to music and sung as hymns. These lines are taken from a longer poem entitled "The Eternal Goodness," written in 1867. Thomas Tallis's *The Third Tune*, composed around 1565 and best known in Ralph Vaughan Williams's 1910 *Fantasia on a Theme* by Thomas Tallis, would be a splendid musical setting for this text.

*I bow my forehead to the dust, I veil mine eyes for shame,*
*and urge, in trembling self-distrust, a prayer without a claim.*
*No offering of my own I have, nor works my faith to prove;*
*I can but give the gifts God gave, and plead his love for love.*

This hymn appeared in sixty-four denominational and other hymnals in the century prior to 1960 but has not appeared in a single hymnal since (it is only available in *The Cyber Hymnal* now). I think I know why. Especially in the opening stanza, the hymn is deeply penitential. But penitence has fallen out of fashion. Millions of voters prefer candidates who bellow their brilliance; admitting to a mistake can end a politician's career. Many modern parents tell their children how wonderful they are (no change necessary) rather than urge them to amend their ways, learn better behaviors, and improve themselves. If God is mentioned at all, it's the God of Elizabeth Gilbert in *Eat, Pray, Love*: "God dwells within you as you yourself, exactly the way you are." Except perhaps in twelve-step groups, self-examination, confession, and reform have become passé.

Penitence can be overdone. God does not ask us to be perpetual grovelers, and whatever else it may be, Christian faith should be joyful—joyful but not arrogant or vain. Christian joy is truthful, and the truth requires acknowledging that we have sinned, the spirit of the age notwithstanding.

My childhood occurred just as that tide was turning. My parents reprimanded me when I needed it and urged me to study more diligently, work harder, and become a better person. I usually obeyed them—I didn't cuss, did my homework, and always addressed my elders as "Sir" and "Ma'am." What more could my parents—or God—want? I wasn't taught to be smug, but I took my parents to mean that if I worked at it, I could become an exemplary boy. Perfection, or at least superiority (and applause), was within reach. I had much to offer that God would surely like.

Years later, after I had fallen on my face several times, I discovered that my best efforts may not be noticed and even when they are, they often amount to little. Occasionally I even needed to "veil mine eyes for shame." The only thing I have to offer God is myself—what God first gave to me—and although I've tarnished it, it's all God wants from me.

*I dimly guess, from blessings known, of greater out of sight;*
*and, with the chastened psalmist, own God's judgments too are right.*
*And if my heart and flesh are weak to bear an untried pain,*
*the bruisèd reed God will not break, but strengthen and sustain.*

Every morning I thank God for my undeserved blessings. If you count your blessings rather than your misfortunes, there will be plenty to count and you will come to see them as indicative of a loving God. Having experienced God as the fount of goodness in the past, you will be confident of further goodness in the future. You will dimly guess, "from blessings known, of greater out of sight." Your universe will have a smiling face.

There will be, of course, pain and suffering. Some people break under that weight, perhaps sedating themselves with alcohol or some other drug, sacrificing mental clarity and good judgment for momentary relief. Others, however, seem able to endure anything without breaking. Those who focus on their blessings and connect their suffering to a value or reality beyond themselves are the most likely to endure suffering without breaking. They look away from themselves to a loving God.

*I know not what the future hath of marvel or surprise,*
*assured alone that life and death God's mercy underlies.*
*And so beside the silent sea I wait the muffled oar:*
*no harm from God can come to me on ocean or on shore.*

My wife keeps a small counted cross-stitch on her dresser that says, "If you want to make God laugh, tell him your plans." I know the truth of that. When I have envisioned a plan for my life, or even for the next week, an unanticipated something (God?) has often intervened to turn me in a different direction—and sometimes taught me lessons I didn't know I needed to learn. The only thing certain about the future is that it will be surprising.

Has God been directing my life from offstage? I'm not sure about that—my sense is that I have freely made choices along the way. But looking back on seven decades, I can say that God's mercy undergirded every year, even (especially?) the years I was most confused and demoralized. I learned to surrender the future to God's merciful hands only when all other choices had been snatched from me.

So will I entrust to God's mercy the time remaining to me? Maybe. It depends on how well I have learned the lessons of the past. But either way, at the end will be God's mercy.

I suppose the "silent sea" and "muffled oar" refer to death's habit of slipping up on us unannounced. Death is a natural thing, even a good thing. Why should I stick around for centuries? Who would want or need my sage advice? Better to move gracefully out of the way and leave advising to others.

*I know not where God's islands lift their fronded palms in air;*
*I only know I cannot drift beyond his love and care.*
*And thou, O Lord, by whom are seen thy creatures as they be,*
*forgive me if too close I lean my human heart on thee.*

I ran across the following passage from American author Ram Dass's *Grist for the Mill*: "As we get close to dying, we start to get very frightened and we start to push pretty hard. We say, 'Doctor, you've got new pills, use them, do anything, save me, freeze-dry me, do anything, I don't want to die,' and grab and hold the bedsheets and pay more and more and get more and more hysterical and get into intensive care units and keep alive even if they have to transplant everything. But no matter how hard we try, suddenly we're dead. And then a voice says to us, 'Hello.'"

Apart from the voice that says "Hello," I don't want any of that. That kind of death hardly suggests a "silent sea" or a "muffled" anything. There comes a time when we need to step aside to make room for those who come after us. When my time comes, I hope my children, grandchildren, and friends (if I am still young enough to have friends) will love me as I love them and then let me go where my forebears have gone before and where they all will someday join me.

 **PRAYER**

Lord, I find it unsettling, even alarming, that you see your "creatures as they be." There is much I'd like to hide from you, and I am so accustomed to wanting to look good that it's almost as if pretending has become part of who I am. Yet you know otherwise. You know exactly who I am.

But you have not abandoned me. You come to me in the person of your Son Jesus. You walk alongside me, pick me up when I stumble, turn me back when I stray, sit with me when I need refreshment, heal me when I grow ill, defend me when the evil one approaches, and prepare for me a resting place at journey's end. Even when I am distracted and you are far from my thoughts, I am not far from your thoughts. You are there beside me, neither slumbering nor sleeping. You are ever vigilant on my behalf, my shield, my advocate, my balm.

Be especially vigilant for me, Lord, as my death approaches. May I greet it willingly, peacefully, and thankfully, and forgive me if "too close I lean my human heart on thee."

*Amen.*

# 17

## I SOUGHT THE LORD

Anonymous, nineteenth century         Suggested tune: *Faith*

*I sought the Lord, and afterward I knew*
*he moved my soul to seek him, seeking me;*
*it was not I that found, O Savior true;*
*no, I was found of thee.*

*Thou didst reach forth thy hand and mine enfold;*
*I walked and sank not on the storm-vexed sea;*
*'twas not so much that I on thee took hold,*
*as thou, dear Lord, on me.*

*I find, I walk, I love, but oh, the whole*
*of love is but my answer, Lord, to thee;*
*for thou wert long beforehand with my soul,*
*always thou lovedst me.*

This anonymous text expresses the author's trusting
confidence in God, suggesting a young child walking hand-
in-hand with a loving guardian across a stormy sea. The
hymn may recall Jesus' walking on the sea and stretching out
his hand to Peter in Matthew 14:22-33. *Faith* was written for
this text by Harold Moyer, a Mennonite hymnal editor, and
first published in 1965.

———∞∞∞———

*I sought the Lord, and afterward I knew*
*he moved my soul to seek him, seeking me;*
*it was not I that found, O Savior true;*
*no, I was found of thee.*

For most of my life I searched for God. When as a young man
I began to wonder about human destiny and the meaning
of life, I wanted answers and began searching—for God,
Ultimate Reality, the Ground of Being, or Someone or
Something that would point me to the answers.

My search drove me to seminary where I ingested lots of
intellectual ideas. Surely I could find the answers there, I
thought. But the more I read, the more confused I became.
I initially held back from making any religious or vocational
commitment because I didn't know what I thought a teacher
or pastor should know. Perhaps one reason I finally decided
to seek ordination was the idea that it would afford me the
opportunity to keep reading and searching for answers.

I still read theology and spiritual literature but not to answer
my questions. There is something better than answered
questions, and I have found it—or rather, it has found me.
Following tradition and for lack of a better word, I call
it God. I wasn't ready to let God find me so long as I was
determined to find God. Maybe my searching for all those
years was God preparing me to receive him one day later on.
Perhaps God allured me, "moved my soul to seek him," until
I finally realized it wasn't about me and my questions—it was

about God, who doesn't deal in answers to questions. God deals in love. When I finally stopped searching, God was there and found me. God had been there all along, but first I had to admit I was lost.

> Thou didst reach forth thy hand and mine enfold;
> I walked and sank not on the storm-vexed sea;
> 'twas not so much that I on thee took hold,
> as thou, dear Lord, on me.

God surely could have taken hold of me all along. But it's hard to take hold of someone who is thrashing and flailing around, and God chose to wait until I had come to the point of exhaustion, until pride and ambition no longer stood in the way and I was willing to be taken hold of.

Psalm 131 perfectly expresses this dependence on a loving God. I pray it regularly these days:

> O LORD, I am not proud;
>     I have no haughty looks.
> I do not occupy myself with great matters,
>     or with things that are too hard for me.
> But I still my soul and make it quiet,
> like a child upon its mother's breast;
>     my soul is quieted within me.
> O Israel, wait upon the LORD,
>     from this time forth for evermore.

Once I had invited God to reach forth his hand and mine enfold, "I walked and sank not on the storm-vexed sea." The storms that tossed me were largely (though not entirely) intellectual in nature, and I regard myself as blessed in that regard. Others are tossed by more daunting storms—poverty, oppression, violence, abuse, illness, disability, loneliness. I pray that they too may learn to be still and let God enfold their hand in his. And if it may be, let me be an instrument through which God takes hold of them as he has taken hold of me.

> I find, I walk, I love, but oh, the whole
> of love is but my answer, Lord, to thee;
> for thou wert long beforehand with my soul,
> always thou lovedst me.

Find, walk, love. Perhaps that is always the sequence. First we find God (or God finds us, as this hymn says) and that usually takes a while. Then we begin to walk with God—walk, not run. The walking will often be at a leisurely pace, and sometimes we must be still, simply *being* with God and not moving at all. The psalmists often speak of waiting on the Lord. To wait patiently is to acknowledge that God is doing what God does, at God's pace. Saint Paul speaks of running the race (I Corinthians 9:24; Galatians 2:2; Philippians 2:16), but as he grew older and after he was incarcerated, I hope he discovered the joy of walking quietly with the Lord, even of waiting patiently. Paul's epistle to the Philippians, written from prison, suggests that this was so. Waiting is sometimes all a prison inmate can do.

As we walk and wait with God, we begin to love God, a love that grows deeper with time and which, we are told, will grow forever deeper, never reaching its limit because we will have entered the realm of a love that is infinite. This is not our love of God, but God's love of us, to which our love is but an echo.

## PRAYER

Thank you, gracious and surprising Lord, for reaching out
your hand to me after I had labored so long to find you. Were
you there all along, calling to me, but I was too distracted by
my searching to hear you? Was my mind so crammed with
ideas about you that there was no room for you yourself?
Were you prodding me, nudging me to the point where
I would stop and look up to see you? And would I have
ever turned to you had I not become so dispirited by my
protracted search?

I wonder about those questions, Lord, but you have taught
me not to linger over unanswerable questions. Rather, I am
to accept your gift of yourself and enjoy your company as I
live each new day. And when I reach my final day, may I place
my hand in yours one more time, and may my surrender to
you be complete at last.

*Amen.*

# 18

## IMMORTAL, INVISIBLE, GOD ONLY WISE

Walter C. Smith (1824-1908)                    Suggested tune: *St. Denio*

Immortal, invisible, God only wise,
in light inaccessible hid from our eyes,
most blessèd, most glorious, the Ancient of Days,
Almighty, victorious, thy great Name we praise.

Unresting, unhasting, and silent as light,
nor wanting, nor wasting, thou rulest in might;
thy justice, like mountains, high soaring above
thy clouds, which are fountains of goodness and love.

To all, life thou givest, to both great and small;
in all life thou livest, the true life of all;
we blossom and flourish like leaves on a tree,
then wither and perish—but naught changeth thee.

Great Father of glory, pure Father of light,
thine angels adore thee, all veiling their sight;
all laud we would render: O help us to see
'tis only the splendor of light hideth thee.

Most holy, most hidden, thine own we would be.
Thou comest: in Jesus our souls rest in thee.
All giving, all loving, we gratefully raise,
on earth and in heaven, our anthems of praise.

This hymn is based on I Timothy 1:17: "To the King of the ages, immortal, invisible, the only God, be honor and glory forever and ever." In most hymnals, the original's five stanzas are condensed into four. I have added a new fifth stanza. The hymn writer, Walter C. Smith, was a pastor and sometime moderator in the Free Church of Scotland. *St. Denio* is based on traditional Welsh ballad tunes.

*Immortal, invisible, God only wise,*
*in light inaccessible hid from our eyes,*
*most blessèd, most glorious, the Ancient of Days,*
*Almighty, victorious, thy great name we praise.*

Early twentieth-century author and scholar Alfred Edward Bailey calls this hymn an "attempt to express the inexpressible" and hence "a stimulus to the imagination." It could well serve as the theme music for the film version of Rudolf Otto's 1917 classic *The Idea of the Holy.* The hymn arises out of the experience of God described in that book. While acknowledging the rational and moral aspects of faith, Otto focuses on what he sees as the fundamental religious impulse, an awareness of what he calls the *numinous.* The term refers to a reality of boundless majesty and energy totally beyond human understanding. The *numinous* is mysterious and stupefying; it is tremendous, inducing fear and dread; and it is fascinating, alluring those who tremble before it.

While Otto's book is an academic text, the hymn is an act of praise by worshipers experiencing the *numinous.* The opening stanza piles divine attribute on attribute, contrasting God (or as Otto would say, the *numinous*) to human beings. It begins with negative attributes: God is not this, not that—not mortal, not visible, not limited in knowledge, not accessible. One feels cowed by a God that is utterly transcendent, totally other, essentially and infinitely distant, never connecting with people.

The stanza then praises this transcendent God as blessed and glorious. There follows yet another attribute—God is "almighty," subject to no higher power. But then God is called victorious, suggesting that despite God's inaccessible otherness, God is engaged in a battle—but against whom or what? We're not told. We are left trembling, prostrate, befuddled, and yet drawn to an unknowable reality engaged in a battle that presumably involves us. We're tantalized, left hanging. Is that it, or is there more?

> *Unresting, unhasting, and silent as light,*
> *nor wanting, nor wasting, thou rulest in might;*
> *thy justice, like mountains, high soaring above*
> *thy clouds, which are fountains of goodness and love.*

The second stanza begins where the first leaves off, with more negative divine attributes: God does not rest, hurry, make noise, need anything, or waste anything. But God has energy; God moves. We're then told that God "rulest in might." All that the hymn has told us about God so far would fit with Otto's *numinous.* We're still left trembling, prostrate, befuddled, and fascinated. Is that it, or is there more?

Suddenly the hymn takes a turn: we find ourselves singing of God's justice "like mountains, high soaring above," of

fountains brimming with "goodness and love." This is not
the language of transcendence. There's more to God than the
distant, unknowable *numinous*. Justice, goodness, and love
are relationship words. They suggest someone—a person or
something like a person—who is engaged with other persons,
who has values, who cares. If seeking a pronoun to refer to
the *numinous*, the only fitting one would seem to be it, but
this stanza suggests something more personal—He? She?
They? We haven't abandoned or denied the *numinous* and
we're still a long way from the God of Jewish, Christian, and
Muslim experience, but we have clearly moved beyond a God
totally remote and inscrutable.

Justice, goodness, and love are concepts drawn from human
experience, so if used when speaking of God, they must
be radically redefined. We will not be the ones doing the
redefining, and we may be startled and caught up short at
what these concepts come to mean when we see what the
transcendent God is doing.

> To all, life thou givest, to both great and small;
> in all life thou livest, the true life of all;
> we blossom and flourish like leaves on a tree,
> then wither and perish—but naught changeth thee.

In the third stanza, we sing of God as the source of life, of
things mutable and passing. That includes us: "we blossom
and flourish like leaves on a tree, then wither and perish."
This is another way of addressing the contrast between Otto's
*numinous*—undying, mysterious, tremendous, and fascinating—
and human beings who die and are at least potentially
understandable, weak, and (often) not so interesting.

Science confirms our seeming insignificance. Astronomers and astrophysicists estimate the age of the observable universe to be 13.8 billion years. If that were compressed into one year, all of recorded history would have occurred in the last fifteen seconds. A human lifespan would be about a seventh of a second.

Or think of it spatially. Those same astronomers and astrophysicists tell us the size of the observable universe from one edge to the other is 93 billion light years (there's some difference of opinion about that, but 93 billion light years is a good guess). In terms of miles, that's 55 followed by 22 zeros. If you compressed that distance into 25,000 miles (the circumference of the Earth), the distance from the Earth to the sun becomes less than a quarter of an inch, and the circumference of the Earth becomes about one fourteen-hundredth of an inch. The height of an average human being would be—well, I can't even figure that out. It seems we are not major figures in the big picture.

This can be depressing, even terrifying. We don't like the thought that not only we ourselves but also everything we accomplish will pass away like a leaf, noticed for a moment, then forgotten, and that even during our fleeting existence we are too small to make any major mark. It makes our lives seem so insignificant, so pointless.

> Great Father of glory, pure Father of light,
> thine angels adore thee, all veiling their sight;
> all laud we would render: O help us to see
> 'tis only the splendor of light hideth thee.

But then, in the fourth stanza, all that is upended. God becomes unabashedly personal: the word Father is twice repeated in the first line. God is not (yet) a human person but can be addressed with one of the most intimate words in human language. Fatherhood is given a new meaning, and human fatherhood now has a new type. God himself (no longer itself) has redefined what it means to be a parent.

But the *numinous* is not diminished. Heavenly beings continue to adore God, still "veiling their sight." We, tiny creatures that we are, dare not do less in our adoration, and it is still true that "the splendor of light hideth thee."

> *Most holy, most hidden, thine own we would be.*
> *Thou comest: in Jesus our souls rest in thee.*
> *All giving, all loving, we gratefully raise,*
> *on earth and in heaven, our anthems of praise.*

As usually sung today, this hymn ends after stanza four. For Jews and Muslims, that's probably satisfactory, but for Christians, there is one more chapter to the story: the *numinous* assumed human flesh at a particular moment in history, at a particular place on this little dot of a planet, and nothing has been the same since. So I have added this fifth stanza of my own writing, as a (hopefully less awkward) Christological coda to this great text. The mysterious, tremendous, and fascinating God is utterly beyond us and yet not inaccessible after all, having chosen to come to us in a manner we can understand and embrace. It isn't anything we had any right or reason to expect, but then, God is not bound by our expectations. In Jesus now our souls rest; we gratefully sing our anthems of praise.

Walter Smith, this hymn's author, included a reference to the incarnation in his fifth and final stanza that is omitted from most modern hymnals, perhaps because the wording seems awkward. It included these words: "And so let thy glory, Almighty, impart, through Christ in his story, thy Christ to the heart."

## PRAYER

Lord God, how can it be that you hear and heed my prayer? Who am I that you should be mindful of me? I will soon vanish like a puff of wind, as will everyone and everything I know. I will be remembered no more. Except by you—you will remember me, even treasure me.

How can this be, Lord God, when you are everything that I am not, the absolutely Other? Even when I ponder the majesty of the heavens, I do not approach you, for the heavens too will pass away. You alone are everlasting. You alone are self-sufficient, dependent on nothing outside yourself. You alone call into being what is not. You alone. You alone. You alone.

And yet you come to me in the person of your Son Jesus, so while I cannot approach you in your infinite and glorious essence, you have approached me, humbling yourself to walk by my side. It seems so unlike the absolutely, almighty Other, "unresting, unhasting, and silent as light, nor wanting, nor wasting," who "rulest in might." But if you are almighty, you alone determine who you are and you do what you wish. You determine everything. I just don't understand why you choose to be who you are and why you have done what you have done. Lord God, how can it be that you hear and heed my prayer?

*Amen.*

# 19

# IT CAME UPON A MIDNIGHT CLEAR

Edmund H. Sears (1810-1876)                    Suggested tune: *Carol*

*It came upon a midnight clear, that glorious song of old,*
*from angels bending near the earth to touch their harps of gold:*
*"Peace on the earth, good will to men,*
  *from heaven's all gracious King."*
*The world in solemn stillness lay to hear the angels sing.*

*Still through the cloven skies they come*
  *with peaceful wings unfurled,*
*and still their heavenly music floats o'er all the weary world;*
*above its sad and lowly plains they bend on hovering wing,*
*and ever o'er its Babel sounds the blessed angels sing.*

*Yet with the woes of sin and strife the world has suffered long;*
*beneath the heavenly hymn have rolled two thousand years of wrong;*
*and warring humankind hears not the tidings which they bring;*
*O hush the noise and cease your strife and hear the angels sing!*

*For lo! the days are hastening on, by prophets seen of old,*
*when with the ever-circling years shall come the time foretold,*
*when peace shall over all the earth its ancient splendors fling,*
*and all the world give back the song which now the angels sing.*

This Christmas carol is unusual in making no reference to the birth of Christ, instead focusing entirely on the angels' song. It was written in 1849 when the clouds of the Civil War were gathering, and New England was experiencing the social upheaval of the Industrial Revolution. Edmund H. Sears was a Unitarian minister in Massachusetts. The tune *Carol* was composed by New York composer and music critic Richard Storrs Willis and published in 1850.

*It came upon a midnight clear, that glorious song of old,*
*from angels bending near the earth to touch their harps of gold:*
*"Peace on the earth, good will to men,*
*    from heaven's all gracious King."*
*The world in solemn stillness lay to hear the angels sing.*

It must have been "a midnight clear" when the shepherds in the fields heard the angels sing. It's hard to imagine the scene against a drizzly or stormy sky. I can see the angels surrounded by stars, illumined by a full moon, bending down, touching the earth with their harps of gold and singing the good news of peace.

But I don't see the world lying in "solemn stillness." Rather, I expect the cacophony of human voices drowned out the angels' song. If the world had lain in stillness, surely more than a few isolated shepherds would have heard it and the good news would have been widely welcomed. The event went unnoticed and unreported.

*Still through the cloven skies they come*
*with peaceful wings unfurled,*
*and still their heavenly music floats o'er all the weary world;*
*above its sad and lowly plains they bend on hovering wing,*
*and ever o'er its Babel sounds the blessed angels sing.*

Where is this heavenly peace? Was it a dreamy illusion? Were the angels mistaken, or did they sing of real peace? It's tempting to say it was an illusion, but there are glimpses of heavenly peace for those with eyes to see. I rarely experience it in the big events. It's in the little places and among the little people that the heavenly peace is glimpsed, in people coping courageously with adversity, graciously caring for someone hard to love, putting their own needs aside for a broader good, stopping to help a beggar, listening to someone no one else has time for. Heavenly peace shines out from those people. They are the ones who hear—and sing—the angels' song. Yes, much of the world is weary, its plains sad and lowly, and its sounds a senseless babble. But over this very world, angels hover and heavenly music floats. The choice of what to hear and what songs to sing is a daily decision.

Cynical persons will say, "The world is dog-eat-dog and the meanest or richest or best-connected dog wins. It's all in the luck of the draw. You're naïve if you think it's any other way. So get what you can while you can. Then you die and somebody else comes after you and it repeats all over again. That's the way it is. Get used to it." I make a conscious decision every day not to listen to those "Babel sounds."

Instead, I listen for angel songs. They can be harder to hear than the Babel sounds, but we can hear them—even in this weary world—if we tune our minds to their frequency. As Saint Paul said: "Whatever is true, whatever is honorable, whatever is just, whatever is pure, whatever is pleasing, whatever is commendable, if there is any excellence and if there is anything worthy of praise, think about these things" (Philippians 4:8). We choose the music we listen to and the songs we sing. Decide to listen for the heavenly songs; join the angel choir.

> Yet with the woes of sin and strife the world has suffered long;
> beneath the heavenly hymn have rolled two thousand years of
> wrong;
> and warring humankind hears not the tidings which they bring;
> O hush the noise and cease your strife and hear the angels sing!

Withdrawing from "the woes of sin and strife" so that we might listen to the angels seems like a good option. Why not retreat to my comfortable study, close the door, meditate at leisure on the goodness of God, and write books like this one? Didn't Jesus himself often draw apart from the world for prayer?

Yes, but he did so only after a long day immersed in the woes of sin and strife. In fact, the whole Christian story, beginning with Jesus' birth in the little town of Bethlehem, is a tale of God's immersion in sin and strife. The standard telling of the story has God reigning for all eternity in heaven but then deciding to leave that charmed abode to enter a world that has suffered long. God didn't have to do that, for whatever else it may mean to be God, it surely means nobody tells you what to do.

So if God chose to descend to us in a dirty stable and then to engage the dregs of human society on the dusty roads of an

obscure, backcountry province, it is there, not in the privacy
of the study, that God is found and the angel songs are heard.

*For lo! the days are hastening on, by prophets seen of old,*
*when with the ever-circling years shall come the time foretold,*
*when peace shall over all the earth its ancient splendors fling,*
*and all the world give back the song which now the angels sing.*

Here's where faith enters in. What you see is determined
partly by what you're taught to see. I recall a horrid story of
a young boy who ran down the stairs to leap into his father's
arms as the father returned home from work. At the last
moment, the father drew back so that his son crashed to the
floor at his feet. "I told you never to trust anybody!" the
father said. If that young boy grew into a man who saw the
world as a cruel joke, one need not wonder why.

But the son would not have been compelled to repeat his
father's cynicism. What we see around us is not determined
solely by what we've been taught. Our experiences influence
us, but they do not bind us. The boy in the story would have
choices later on and may have chosen faith over nihilism. You
can't prove it either way; it's a matter of what you choose to see.

To choose faith is to affirm that the world is not a cruel joke,
that history is not just one damned thing after another, but
has a goal, a direction, a purpose. The days are hastening
on and the time foretold will come, "when peace shall over
all the earth its ancient splendors fling, and all the world
give back the song which now the angels sing." Choose it.
Embrace it. Live it.

## PRAYER

I'm listening, Lord. Let me hear the angels' songs and then let me join with all my heart in singing them.

*Amen.*

# 20

## JESUS, LOVER OF MY SOUL

Charles Wesley (1707-1788)                    Suggested tune: *Aberystwyth*

Jesus, lover of my soul, let me to thy bosom fly,
while the nearer waters roll, while the tempest still is high;
hide me, O my Savior, hide, till the storm of life is past;
safe into the haven guide, O receive my soul at last!

Other refuge have I none; hangs my helpless soul on thee;
leave, ah! leave me not alone, still support and strengthen me.
All my trust on thee is stayed, all my help from thee I bring;
cover my defenseless head with the shadow of thy wing.

Thou, O Christ, art all I want, more than all in thee I find:
Raise the fallen, cheer the faint, heal the sick, and lead the blind.
Just and holy is thy name, I am all unrighteousness;
false and full of sin I am, thou art full of truth and grace.

Plenteous grace with thee is found, grace to cover all my sin;
let the healing streams abound; make and keep me pure within.
Thou of life the fountain art; freely let me take of thee;
spring thou up within my heart, rise to all eternity.

This may be Charles Wesley's most popular hymn, sung
the world over. The third stanza, seeming to suggest the
unpopular (because it is misunderstood) Calvinist teaching
of the total depravity of man, is omitted in some hymnals.
Even with this stanza, however, Charles Wesley was hardly
a Calvinist. Like the hymn as a whole, the third stanza
expresses Wesley's sense that he is helpless and unworthy of
the love Christ so bountifully bestows upon him. The rugged
tune *Aberystwyth* was composed by the nineteenth-century
Welsh musician Joseph Parry.

*Jesus, lover of my soul, let me to thy bosom fly,*
*while the nearer waters roll, while the tempest still is high;*
*hide me, O my Savior, hide, till the storm of life is past;*
*safe into the haven guide, O receive my soul at last!*

A probably apocryphal story is told about the writing of
this hymn. It's said that Charles Wesley was at the seashore
when a violent storm arose. A foundering ship could be seen
offshore with passengers on deck terrified for their lives.
Suddenly a small bird flew through Wesley's open window,
buffeted by the wind and rain and pursued by a hawk. The
bird flew into Wesley's lap and found safety in the folds of
his shirt. Some have said this incident suggested this hymn
to Wesley. The story has the ring of a sentimental legend,
but it's a fact that Wesley nearly died in a great storm on the
Atlantic in 1736 as he returned to England from a stint as a
missionary to St. Simons Island, Georgia. If any incident in
his life led to the composing of this hymn, written in 1739, it

was likely that one. In any case, the hymn's vivid images of a refuge in the storm have spoken to generations of Christians.

The hymn reminds me of the psalm that the anonymous author of Jonah puts into Jonah's mouth as he languishes in the belly of the fish (Jonah 2:3). Jonah even sees the Lord as having thrown him into the stormy sea: "You cast me into the deep, into the heart of the seas, and the flood surrounded me; all your waves and your billows passed over me." Many people humbled by events, perhaps of their own doing but beyond their control, eventually come to see the hand of God in those events.

I've never been in a storm at sea, but I have felt storm-tossed in other ways. Some of those storms arose from within me—nagging doubts, fear of failing, faceless dreads. Other storms resulted from foolish decisions on my part or the behavior of others. While I wouldn't say that God caused those storms or threw me into the midst of them—I acted of my own free will—I believe God was standing nearby, knowing it would take some kind of storm to drive me into his arms. Then I found in his bosom the promised safe haven that received my soul at last. God is willing to wait until we are ready to turn to him.

> Other refuge have I none; hangs my helpless soul on thee;
> leave, ah! leave me not alone, still support and strengthen me.
> All my trust on thee is stayed, all my help from thee I bring;
> cover my defenseless head with the shadow of thy wing.

People seek refuge, or at least satisfaction, in all sorts of places—in work, material assets, alcohol, food, education, sex, earning a good reputation. Some of those things are satisfying, for a time. But at the end of the day, they leave us still feeling insecure and threatened. Bad things happen. We are laid off. Marriages fail. Friends betray our confidences. Colleagues misunderstand us. Loved ones die or move away. Natural disasters wipe out entire communities.

The sting of these storm-like events is tempered when we discover that Christ is there, usually in the form of another person who cares. God can bring good out of evil. Pain can teach endurance. Betrayal can teach forgiveness. Poverty can teach how to live simply. Immobility can provide time for prayer and reflection. What we make of adversity is our choice.

It was from a dark prison cell, surrounded by rodents and insects, that Saint Paul wrote to the Philippians, "Rejoice in the Lord always....The Lord is near. Do not worry about anything...and the peace of God, which surpasses all understanding, will guard your hearts and your minds in Christ Jesus" (Philippians 4:4-7).

*Thou, O Christ, art all I want, more than all in thee I find:*
*Raise the fallen, cheer the faint, heal the sick, and lead the blind.*
*Just and holy is thy name, I am all unrighteousness;*
*false and full of sin I am, thou art full of truth and grace.*

It's not true that "Thou, O Christ, art all I want." I do want Christ—I would even say I long for Christ—but I want much else besides. Nor do I think it wrong that I want other things in addition to Christ. The things I want are what everyone wants: love, friendship, food and shelter, health, useful work to do, something of beauty in my life. If ever there were a person who didn't want these things, would that person be truly human?

If "I am all unrighteousness...false and full of sin" (a description I don't reject), it isn't because I want what every human being wants. It's because I place my desire for those things ahead of following Christ. I seek those things before I seek to "raise the fallen, cheer the faint, heal the sick, and lead the blind." The hymn envisions Christ doing those things, but through what agent does he do them if not through me? And if I am so distracted by lesser desires that the fallen are not raised, the faint are not cheered, the sick are not healed, and the blind are not led, can I honestly claim to be Christ's disciple?

*Plenteous grace with thee is found, grace to cover all my sin;*
*let the healing streams abound; make and keep me pure within.*
*Thou of life the fountain art; freely let me take of thee;*
*spring thou up within my heart, rise to all eternity.*

"Plenteous grace" occurs when the storms and floods that frighten us are transformed into "healing streams," the fountain of life that sustains us. That typically happens when we are ready for it to happen, when we have exhausted all other possibilities. God usually (I would never say always) gives plenteous grace only to those who are spiritually prepared to receive it, and the best posture to receive it is flat on our backs, a posture few of us assume until circumstances compel us to do so.

## — ⚬⚬⚬ — PRAYER — ⚬⚬⚬ —

But for you, O Christ, I am blown helplessly in the wind.
All my life I have been told of your promise that you will
not abandon me, and my experience seems to confirm it.
You have plucked me from many a danger. When I speak of
the times when I prayed to you and you came to me, Jesus,
someone will often say that maybe it wasn't you at all; maybe
I would have weathered the storm regardless, and I begin
to think that way. Fickle and unreliable as I am, "false and
full of sin," I don't deserve your attention, Jesus. Why would
you give me even a passing nod of the head? Yet you remain
my hope. Cut off from you, I would be left in the void with
only my own ruminations to comfort me. "Leave, ah! Leave
me not alone! All my trust on thee is stayed." I trust you,
O Christ, to form me—to re-form me—into the person you
envision me to be.

"Cover my defenseless head with the shadow of thy wing," O
Christ. Hold me close to your breast, as a mother hen gathers
her chicks unto her. Warmed by your feathers, let me feel your
breath and heartbeat, secure and protected by your love and
power. There shall I find rest from my exhaustion, and there
may I sing your praises, thank and glorify you, all my days.

*Amen.*

# 21

## JOY DAWNED AGAIN ON EASTER DAY

Fourth or fifth century                    Suggested tune: *Puer nobis nascitur*
tr. John Mason Neale (1818-1866)

*Joy dawned again on Easter Day,*
*the sun shone out with fairer ray,*
*when, to their longing eyes restored,*
*the apostles saw their risen Lord.*

*His risen flesh with radiance glowed;*
*his wounded hands and feet he showed:*
*those scars their silent witness gave*
*that Christ was risen from the grave.*

*O Jesus, King of gentleness,*
*do thou our inmost hearts possess;*
*and we to thee will ever raise*
*the tribute of our grateful praise.*

*Jesus, who art the Lord of all,*
*in this our Easter festival,*
*from every weapon death can wield*
*thine own redeemed, thy people, shield.*

*All praise, O risen Lord, we give*
*to thee, who, dead, again dost live;*
*to God the Father equal praise,*
*and God the Holy Ghost, we raise.*

This hymn, written in Latin, is traditionally ascribed to Ambrose of Milan (ca. 335-397), though that authorship has been questioned. *Puer nobis nascitur* dates from the fifteenth century but may be based on a folk tune from an earlier time.

*Joy dawned again on Easter Day,*
*the sun shone out with fairer ray,*
*when, to their longing eyes restored,*
*the apostles saw their risen Lord.*

Joy wasn't the first emotion that dawned on Easter Day. The original version of the Gospel of Mark ends like this: "They went out and fled from the tomb; for terror and amazement had seized them; and they said nothing to anyone, for they were afraid." That's not surprising. I can't imagine anyone bursting into song upon finding a tomb suddenly missing its corpse. And then the corpse comes back to life? Hardly a cheery thought. It took some time for the joy of Easter to dawn on the disciples.

But dawn it did. That very night the apostles saw their risen Lord in a room where they had secluded themselves out of fear. Jesus said, "Peace be with you. As the Father has sent me, so I send you" (John 20:21). He put the disciples' fears to rest and gave them a peace I doubt they had ever experienced before. He also gave them a mission—something to do—and the Holy Spirit to empower them to do it. Christ's resurrection turned everything upside down. What had been a demoralizing defeat became an astonishing, energizing victory.

*His risen flesh with radiance glowed;*
*his wounded hands and feet he showed:*
*those scars their silent witness gave*
*that Christ was risen from the grave.*

One of the disciples was not present when Jesus appeared and gave the disciples his peace that evening of Easter Day (John 20:24-29). We're not told where Thomas was, but he was not with the others. When Thomas returned, he understandably doubted what they told him and said he would believe it only if he could see the imprint of the nails in Jesus' hands and place his hand in the side of Jesus where the spear had wounded him.

Jesus appeared to the disciples again a week later, and this time Thomas was present. Jesus didn't rebuke or condemn Thomas. Rather, he gave the disciples his peace again and then invited Thomas to touch him, to place his fingers and hands into his wounds. "Do not doubt but believe," he told Thomas. Thomas's response was short and to the point: "My Lord and my God!"

*O Jesus, King of gentleness,*
*do thou our inmost hearts possess;*
*and we to thee will ever raise*
*the tribute of our grateful praise.*

Jesus' resurrection from the dead couldn't have been a "gentle" event. It suggests an unfathomable power, initially frightening, then inspiring, and eventually joyful, but never gentle. Jesus' life on earth also suggests a stupendous power—casting out demons, calming a storm, raising the dead. But in Jesus' earthly life we also see the gentleness of which this hymn speaks. He was powerful, yet gentle.

I am reminded of my maternal grandmother, whose love for me seemed to know no bounds. Such was her power over me that she could get me to do whatever she wanted by simply mentioning it. I would have done anything to please her. She exercised her power through gentleness. Her power, in fact, derived from her gentleness, and her spirit took up residence within me as well. "Do thou our inmost hearts possess," we pray, asking Christ to reside in us and make us powerfully gentle as he is powerfully gentle.

*Jesus, who art the Lord of all,*
*in this our Easter festival,*
*from every weapon death can wield*
*thine own redeemed, thy people, shield.*

When we ask Jesus to shield us "from every weapon death can wield," what would those weapons be? Death has several weapons in its arsenal:

- Fear. Many of us fear dying, some because of the pain that often attends dying, some because of what may happen to those left behind, and some because of uncertainty about what lies on the other side.

- Isolation. As death approaches, some people cut themselves off from those who love them. This can result from misplaced pride that resists being dependent on others or from unresolved issues from an earlier time.

- Anger. I have dealt with people who, as death drew near, were so angry that their final days were an ordeal to everyone around them. The anger could be directed at anything or anyone, for any slight, real or imagined. The effect is the same wherever the anger is directed.

- Guilt. Some people go to their graves burdened by debilitating, unresolved guilt. They need to confess and ask forgiveness before dying. Others depart this life with a sense of guilt arising for no apparent reason.

- Regret. We all wish we had done some things differently, but we need not focus on those things at the end of life. Rather, we should focus on our moments of redemption.

The risen Christ can grant us immunity from the weapons death can wield and enable us to put them behind us. Be still, thoughts that know not the power of Christ's resurrection. Trust him.

*All praise, O risen Lord, we give*
*to thee, who, dead, again dost live;*
*to God the Father equal praise,*
*and God the Holy Ghost, we raise.*

Many hymns conclude with a stanza praising the Trinity. It serves as a kind of coda to what has gone before.

## PRAYER

I wish I had been in that room on Easter night, Lord Jesus. Like Thomas, I've often felt like the one left out, the one who wasn't there. Had I been Thomas, I too would have doubted. Part of me doubts even today. I wish you would invite me to see and touch your wounds, but that seems to have been a one-time gift to Thomas only. Why is it so hard for me to believe what others tell me, to see what they see? I long to believe, but something in me wants to dismiss your resurrection as fantasy, a fairy tale, wishful thinking, too good to be true. Dead people don't come back to life, or so I would have insisted. "Blessed are those who have not seen and yet believe," you said. If I am to believe, Lord, it will have to be without having seen, and that's a leap for me.

*"You don't understand about believing, Dick. It's not like believing that the sun will set tonight or that George Washington was the first president of the United States. You believe the sun will set because it's always set before, and you believe about George Washington because you've been told about him. This is a different kind of believing. It's like believing that Pam loves you and that she will be faithful to you. It's believing in, not believing that. You believe in Pam. You trust her because your experience of her tells you to trust her. What does your experience of me tell you? You haven't seen my wounds, but can you trust me?"*

I remember several times when you have been there for me, Lord, even when I doubted you. Or at least it could have been you. I think it was you. I was dead or as good as dead, and you brought me back to life. Maybe that's proof of the resurrection, but I have no guarantee that my future will be like my past.

*"Proof? Love can't be proven, and did I promise you a guarantee? If there were a guarantee, trust wouldn't be necessary. Trust is a decision and a risk. Will you trust me?"*

I don't know. Some days I trust you, and some days I don't. Part of it is that "King of gentleness" thing. You were gentle with most people, most of the time, especially with the "nobodies"—lepers, Samaritans, publicans, the maimed, the sick, prostitutes, children. The only people you weren't gentle with were the ones who called the shots, those who saw themselves as the "beautiful people." You railed against them, ridiculed them. And you let them kill you! Look where gentleness took you, Lord! Why did you let that happen? Will that happen to me if I trust you?

*"Maybe. I told you there's no guarantee. There may be suffering along the way, injuries and affronts. But contrary to what you see and what the world tells you, gentleness trumps power. That's what my life was about, and it's what the resurrection is about. Blessed are the poor in spirit. Blessed are those who mourn. Blessed are the meek. Love your enemies. Pray for those who persecute you. Do not lay up for yourself treasures on earth. Ask, and it will be given to you. Seek, and you shall find. Knock, and it will be opened to you. Whoever would save his life will lose it, and whoever loses his life for my sake will find it. The last will be first. Appearances aside, there will be victory in the end for the gentle.*

"You had better learn to live with your doubts, for there are things you will never understand, things beyond human telling. But will you trust me? What's important to you? What kind of person do you want to be? Whose side are you on? That's the decision. What do you say?"

Amen.

# 22

# LEAD, KINDLY LIGHT

John Henry Newman (1801-1890)                    Suggested tune: *Lux benigna*

Lead, kindly light, amid the encircling gloom, lead thou me on;
the night is dark, and I am far from home; lead thou me on:
keep thou my feet; I do not ask to see
the distant scene; one step enough for me.

I was not ever thus, nor prayed that thou shouldst lead me on;
I loved to choose and see my path; but now lead thou me on.
I loved the garish day, and, spite of fears,
pride ruled my will: remember not past years.

So long thy power hath blessed me, sure it still will lead me on
o'er moor and fen, o'er crag and torrent, till the night is gone;
and with the morn those angel faces smile
which I have loved long since, and lost awhile.

Meantime, along the narrow rugged path thyself hast trod,
lead, Savior, lead me home in childlike faith, home to my God,
to rest forever after earthly strife
in the calm light of everlasting life.

At the 1893 World Parliament of Religions held in Chicago, representatives of all the world's major faiths met for the first time to seek common ground and mutual understanding. A hymn was sought in which all could join. The first three stanzas of this hymn were chosen since all religious believers seek light "amid the encircling gloom." John Henry Newman was the leading spokesman for the Anglo-Catholic revival in the Church of England until he converted to Roman Catholicism in 1845. He received a cardinal's hat in 1879. *Lux benigna* was composed for this text in 1865 by John Bachus Dykes, an English clergyman.

*Lead, kindly light, amid the encircling gloom, lead thou me on;*
*the night is dark, and I am far from home; lead thou me on:*
*keep thou my feet; I do not ask to see*
*the distant scene; one step enough for me.*

John Henry Newman was thirty-two years old when he wrote these brooding, haunting lines. He was on a ship in the Mediterranean and had fallen ill, probably with malaria, but Newman was also troubled by deeper things. It would be twelve more years before he would leave the Church of England for Rome, but the wrenching spiritual and intellectual struggle leading up to that move had already begun. Newman was confused; he felt lost and alienated, that his soul had entered the shadows. He longed for clarity, for light in his darkness. In this hymn, Newman prays for guidance to a God who may have seemed especially opaque to him at this time. He longs to see "the distant scene," where all will be resolved, but he does not ask to see it, probably knowing that such knowledge is impossible.

The hymn draws upon Newman's reading of Exodus 14 where the Israelites have just escaped from slavery in Egypt, but Pharaoh has reconsidered and his army is in hot pursuit. The Israelites are frightened and disoriented. Then the angel of the Lord, in the form of a pillar of fire, leads the Israelites through the Red Sea to safety. The hymn expresses both Newman's sense of being lost and confused "amid the encircling gloom" and his hope to be led by the "kindly light" into the brightness of a new day.

> I was not ever thus, nor prayed that thou shouldst lead me on;
> I loved to choose and see my path; but now lead thou me on.
> I loved the garish day, and, spite of fears,
> pride ruled my will: remember not past years.

In the second stanza, Newman turns away from his present confusion and looks back on his life. He confesses that, like most youths, he asked for no guidance because he felt no need of it. Spiritual maturity comes only after we have run into some walls and traveled down a few dead-end byways. Then we wake up and discover how little we know about anything.

Like Newman, I have not always sought divine guidance. Years ago, I loved "the garish day" and "pride ruled my will." It seemed the paths before me were infinite in number and all mine for the choosing. I knew even then that to have choices marked me as a privileged young man, for many of my friends saw before them only a numbing necessity they would never have chosen, stretching to the horizon and beyond. But I surveyed a field of choices. Many of the choices I made have brought blessings to me, but some turned sour. It serves no purpose now to wonder how things would have gone had I chosen otherwise, if I had always taken the path of faithfulness. Like most people, my life has been a mixture of the faithful and the unfaithful. "Remember not past years."

> *So long thy power hath blessed me, sure it still will lead me on*
> *o'er moor and fen, o'er crag and torrent, till the night is gone;*
> *and with the morn those angel faces smile*
> *which I have loved long since, and lost awhile.*

This stanza looks forward, acknowledging that there will be moors and fens, crags and torrents, challenges unimaginable, but that finally, if we take one step at a time, led by the kindly light, dawn will come.

As I write these words, I am more than twice Newman's age when he wrote this hymn, but I identify with every word of it. His confusion was apparently resolved later in life, but I continue to live with mine. My vision is often clouded; my faith is largely one of hope. I see the light at times, or think I see it, and at other times I see nothing. Either way, I am learning to take the next step, trusting God to lead me into the future. It's a lesson I haven't fully learned, but it's coming.

> *Meantime, along the narrow rugged path thyself hast trod,*
> *lead, Savior, lead me home in childlike faith, home to my God,*
> *to rest forever after earthly strife*
> *in the calm light of everlasting life.*

I'd like a dose of that "childlike faith," but what would that look like? As a child, I trusted everyone and doubted

nothing; everything seemed clear to me, and there was
some truth in that: I felt loved because I truly was loved; my
position in the large extended family that surrounded me was
never in question.

But as I matured, life's complexities and ambiguities rose
up before me. Doubt invaded my secure little world, and
nothing seemed clear. I was no longer sure who I was or what
I was to do. Eventually, I came to accept that, at least in this
life, much will be opaque to me. A certain humility comes
with this realization, and I believe it is a healthy thing, a
normal part of growing into a mature adult. My childhood
faith was as much childish as childlike. Childish faith fails to
recognize evil; childlike faith trusts in the face of evil.

Now in my old age, I ask for a faith that is childlike but not
childish, and I look forward to taking up residence "after
earthly strife in the calm light of everlasting life" where
childish naïveté and childlike trust will be indistinguishable
because evil will be no more.

## PRAYER

The encircling gloom is sometimes all I see, O God. The
night is dark, and I feel so far from home that it seems I have
no home and will grope forever along these strange back
streets. And yet these are the streets I have known all my life.
Why do they now seem so foreign and foreboding? Is it the
streets or is it me? Perhaps, Lord, these streets glow with
your glory but something in me cannot or will not see it.

So "keep thou my feet," kindly light. Lead thou me on. I am tired of walking into the unknown. If it is unfaithful to ask to see where I am going, then forgive me for asking. Yet Lord, you know how I want to see just a short distance down the road I am to travel, just the next few steps. But if I know you walk with me, I can step forward without knowing where the next step leads, even whether there will be a next step. Make me to know that you are there, O God.

"Remember not past years" except when I repent of my infidelities or thank you for blessings received and woes averted. The ratio of blessings to woes has been skewed in my favor, for I have received at your hand better than I deserve, possibly better than anyone deserves. And even the woes I did not avert were turned to blessings when I allowed them to draw me closer to you.

Stepping blindly into the future is easier now, my God, in old age, for I can now recall occasions when your power has blessed me in the past. The moors and fens, the crags and torrents, have unsettled and frightened me, especially when I felt lost and saw no way out of them. But you knocked me down at the right moment, the moment I was finally ready to stop and take note of you. Then you picked me up, fluffed me like a sat-on pillow, and started me out again in a new direction.

And so I take the next step. I don't know where I'm going and I don't have to know, because you know where I'm going. Be at my side, O God. Trusting in you, I do not ask to see the distant scene. It is enough for me that you see and that you are with me.

*Amen.*

# 23

# LIFT EVERY VOICE AND SING

James Weldon Johnson (1871-1938)                    Tune: *Lift Every Voice*

*Lift every voice and sing till earth and heaven ring,*
*ring with the harmonies of liberty.*
*Let our rejoicing rise high as the listening skies,*
*let it resound loud as the rolling sea.*
*Sing a song full of the faith that the dark past has taught us,*
*sing a song full of the hope that the present has brought us.*
*Facing the rising sun of our new day begun,*
*let us march on till victory is won.*

*Stony the road we trod, bitter the chastening rod,*
*felt in the days when hope unborn had died;*
*yet with a steady beat, have not our weary feet*
*come to the place for which our fathers sighed?*
*We have come over a way that with tears has been watered,*
*we have come, treading our path through the blood of the slaughtered,*
*out from the gloomy past, till now we stand at last*
*where the white gleam of our bright star is cast.*

*God of our weary years, God of our silent tears,*
*thou who hast brought us thus far on the way,*
*thou who hast by thy might led us into the light,*
*keep us forever in the path, we pray.*
*Lest our feet stray from the places, our God, where we met thee,*
*lest, our hearts drunk with the wine of the world, we forget thee;*
*shadowed beneath thy hand, may we forever stand,*
*true to our God, true to our native land.*

African American poet James Weldon Johnson wrote this poem and read it for the first time in 1900 at the segregated Florida school where he served as principal. It was set to music five years later by Johnson's brother, John Rosamond Johnson. It began appearing in hymnals in the late 1970s and is still celebrated today as the black national anthem.

*Lift every voice and sing till earth and heaven ring,*
*ring with the harmonies of liberty.*
*Let our rejoicing rise high as the listening skies,*
*let it resound loud as the rolling sea.*
*Sing a song full of the faith that the dark past has taught us,*
*sing a song full of the hope that the present has brought us.*
*Facing the rising sun of our new day begun,*
*let us march on till victory is won.*

This hymn brims with references to the suffering of African Americans ("the dark past," "the bitter chastening rod," "our silent tears") and their hope for a better future ("the rising sun," "march on till victory is won," "our bright star"). The similarity to the exodus of the ancient Israelites from Egypt stands out like a blinking light.

Most African Americans continue to struggle with the legacy that slavery inflicted on their ancestors. Even today, African Americans often have fewer opportunities than white Americans for a good education, a good job, and a safe neighborhood in which to live. This hymn vividly recalls that "gloomy past" and the continuing struggle to set right the wrongs it continues to inflict on millions of Americans.

*Stony the road we trod, bitter the chastening rod,*
*felt in the days when hope unborn had died;*
*yet with a steady beat, have not our weary feet*
*come to the place for which our fathers sighed?*
*We have come over a way that with tears has been watered,*
*we have come, treading our path through the blood of the slaughtered,*
*out from the gloomy past, till now we stand at last*
*where the white gleam of our bright star is cast.*

Bitter, stony, weary, gloomy—words expressing the cruelty of slavery tumble over one another in this stanza. It does not, however, encourage anger, self-pity, or resignation but resonates with hope for a brighter day.

*God of our weary years, God of our silent tears,*
*thou who hast brought us thus far on the way,*
*thou who hast by thy might led us into the light,*
*keep us forever in the path, we pray.*
*Lest our feet stray from the places, our God, where we met thee,*
*lest, our hearts drunk with the wine of the world, we forget thee;*
*shadowed beneath thy hand, may we forever stand,*
*true to our God, true to our native land.*

Some people forget what their past taught them of God, especially when "the wine of the world" provides sedating comforts. This is nothing new. The Hebrew prophets railed at ancient Israel and Judah for denying hospitality to strangers and oppressing the poor. Had they forgotten that God had saved their ancestors who were refugees wandering in the desert? The early Christians were oppressed and persecuted, but when the church acquired power and prestige in the fourth century, prelates began behaving like entitled aristocrats. Most white Americans are descended from European refugees who fled to this land for freedom, safety, or opportunity, but when modern refugees seek a home here today, some turn them away. And the modern state of Israel was founded as a home for stateless Jews, yet many Israelis refuse to see that they have rendered their Palestinian neighbors stateless today. Forgetting one's past is nothing new.

Yet most African Americans have not forgotten. The laws have been changed but many of the disadvantages and deprivations traceable to their ancestors' servitude remain. That experience can either strangle or strengthen the soul, and we see examples of both among African Americans today. While some turn to drugs, violence, and gang warfare, exacerbating their problems, many others find God amidst their "weary years" and "silent tears," a God more at home in the shack and the hovel than in the stately mansion, a God who entered the world in a cowshed and exited on a cross. This hymn sees adversities as "the places, our God, where we met thee" and pleads that "the wine of the world" not induce forgetfulness. "Keep us forever in the path," the hymn prays.

For people of all races, this hymn keeps the crimes and tragedies of the past before us and challenges us to correct the continuing injustices they have bequeathed us and never to repeat them.

## —∞∞— PRAYER —∞∞—

Is it presumptuous for me to sing this hymn, Lord? As a tall,
white, straight, healthy, educated, comfortably pensioned
male from the American South, I could be the poster boy for
the oppressor class. Never can I recall being discriminated
against or fearful for my life. Now and then, someone
dislikes me, but that is hardly comparable to living with
systemic dangers, deprivations, and indignities. How dare I
even comment on this text, much less sing it?

To my knowledge, dear God, none of my forebears were
slave owners. My German ancestors arrived in America just
after the Civil War had freed the slaves. But I grew up in a
segregated, racist culture in a small Kentucky town in the
1950s. In the totally white neighborhood where I was raised,
we had good schools, while black-skinned children living less
than a mile away did not. Not until I was sixteen years old
did I sit at the same table with an African American boy. That
was in the school cafeteria as our school was beginning to
integrate, and I still remember how uncomfortable it made
me. And yet, black women had been preparing and serving
my food for as long as I could remember. What did I think
might happen if I ate lunch next to an African American?
Why, Lord, did I never question segregated restrooms,
theaters, and restaurants until I was nearly an adult? I was
encouraged to study hard, which I did, and then graduated
from college and graduate school, but I only did what was
expected of me. African American children growing up a few
blocks away from me also did what was expected of them, but
their circumstances dealt them lower expectations, so doing
what was expected didn't take them as far as it took me.

Why was I born where I was and not somewhere else, Lord? Life has dealt me a privileged hand, and I hope I am playing it justly and generously. But how many injustices has my privileged birth blinded me to? What injustices today that I should be seeking to correct do I accept without blinking an eye? Is being born to privilege something of which I should repent? I don't feel guilty—privileged and perhaps obtuse— but not guilty of something that was beyond my control. But if my privileged birth blinds me from seeing what in me needs changing, make me see it, dear God. Open my eyes that I may see as you see and warm my heart that I may love as you love.

I enjoy singing this rousing hymn (even the high F), but when I sing it, may I never forget that I can but faintly understand how deeply it resonates with so many others.

*Amen.*

# 24

# LO! HE COMES
# WITH CLOUDS DESCENDING

Charles Wesley (1707-1788)                Suggested tune: *Helmsley*

*Lo! He comes with clouds descending, once for our salvation slain;*
*thousand, thousand saints attending swell the triumph of his train:*
*Alleluia! Alleluia! Christ the Lord returns to reign.*

*Every eye shall now behold him, robed in dreadful majesty;*
*those who set at nought and sold him, pierced, and nailed him to*
*        the tree,*
*deeply wailing, deeply wailing, shall the true Messiah see.*

*Those dear tokens of his passion still his dazzling body bears,*
*cause of endless exultation to his ransomed worshipers;*
*with what rapture, with what rapture gaze we on those*
*        glorious scars.*

*Yea, amen! let all adore thee, high on thine eternal throne;*
*Savior, take the power and glory; claim the kingdom for thine own:*
*Alleluia! Alleluia! Thou shalt reign, and thou alone.*

"There is nobody like Charles Wesley for packing a volume of pregnant thought into a short hymn," said music scholar Eric Routley. That is certainly true of this hymn, with a biblical reference (or two) in every line. Wesley published it in 1758. *Helmsley* is the tune to which Wesley's brother John originally set this text. John attributed it to one Thomas Olivers, who said it was based on a tune he had heard whistled in the street.

*Lo! He comes with clouds descending, once for our salvation slain;*
*thousand, thousand saints attending swell the triumph of his train:*
*Alleluia! Alleluia! Christ the Lord returns to reign.*

No doubt it was *Helmsley*, a grand, soaring melody of the sort that the renowned English novelist Dorothy Sayers once described as "good, thick stuff," that first attracted me to this hymn. I would probably be thrilled to sing the federal tax code set to this tune.

The text is more problematic for me. Dispensationalists and other Christians of a literalist bent will readily tell you what the Second Coming will entail and sometimes even when it will occur. But that doesn't work for me because the biblical texts about the Second Coming, including the Lord's returning "with clouds descending" (Mark 13:26; Revelation 1:7), are based mainly on dreams and visions. Dreams are symbolic, and symbols are not previews of future events but pertain to deeper things—values, relationships, decisions, desires, anxieties. They often point to great truths but not truths of the sort you'd read about in a newspaper the next day.

The Bible's dream symbols portray a universe embroiled in a war between good and evil. This conflict rages in every age. It calls for a life-or-death decision: Which side are you on? The dreams suggest that faithfulness is not a matter of mere good behavior or correct beliefs. It's a willingness to risk all for what really matters. Are you willing?

But the Second Coming texts are also about the end times, foreseeing a climactic event at the end of history with good triumphing over evil. Don't waste your energy, however, trying to figure out when Christ will return or imagining the specifics of his coming. We are not to know such things. But while we cannot see the future, we can prepare for it. Be vigilant and ready every moment by serving Christ here and now. Is your neighbor hungry? Feed her. Is someone in prison? Visit him. Are people homeless? Open your home to them. Do you have more money than you need? Give it to those who have too little.

> Every eye shall now behold him, robed in dreadful majesty;
> those who set at nought and sold him, pierced, and nailed him to
>     the tree,
> deeply wailing, deeply wailing, shall the true Messiah see.

Why would anyone wail at Christ's return (Matthew 13:42, 50; Revelation 18:15, 19)? Those for whom something else is more important than loving God and neighbor will find Christ's rule intolerable. The returning Messiah issues an open invitation to the heavenly banquet, but some would rather dine elsewhere.

In the parable of the talents (Matthew 25:14-30), the worthless servant is cast into the outer darkness where there is weeping and gnashing of teeth. This is not because his master would not have welcomed him, but because, by his behavior, that servant chose the outer darkness. In the parable of the last judgment (Matthew 25:31-46), we see the Son of man separating the sheep from the goats. The difference between them is that one lives faithfully and the other unfaithfully. Some go to eternal punishment and others to eternal life, but all go where they choose to go.

Could it be that all spend eternity in the same place, where the reign of God causes some to rejoice and others to wail? Do you choose rejoicing or wailing? You are making that choice now.

> *Those dear tokens of his passion still his dazzling body bears,*
> *cause of endless exultation to his ransomed worshipers;*
> *with what rapture, with what rapture gaze we on those*
> *glorious scars.*

It is not Christ's scars that dazzle us but the love that they signify. "Those glorious scars" testify that our God does not sit serenely in heaven while we struggle below but descends to struggle alongside us. It is this wounded, bleeding, scarred Lord, a Lord on intimate terms with suffering, who shall return in glory.

Unlike Jesus, some of us try to avoid scars, and we don't want to look at the scars of others. We prefer an easier, softer way. But how can one who bears no scar claim to be following Christ? The Irish missionary Amy Carmichael has written:

*...as the Master shall the servant be,*
*And piercèd are the feet that follow me;*
*But thine are whole: can he have followed far*
*Who has nor wound nor scar?*

*Yea, amen! let all adore thee, high on thine eternal throne;*
*Savior, take the power and glory; claim the kingdom for thine own:*
*Alleluia! Alleluia! Thou shalt reign, and thou alone.*

This hymn's final stanza contains a hint of what every faithful Christian surely desires—universal salvation—though (so far as we can see) there is no guarantee of it. When Charles Wesley wrote these lines, he probably was not thinking that God's embrace would include everyone, but his text seems to suggest or allow for it. Could it be that someday all created beings, forgiven and redeemed, will gather around the heavenly throne and adore their King? Even Judas Iscariot? Adolf Hitler? Osama bin Laden? Satan himself? I believe Christ never withdraws the invitation to repent and turn to him, that the gate is forever open to all, but some may forever choose to remain outside.

We cannot know whether in the end all will find their intended place in the arms of God, but even the least worthy are welcome. As we anticipate the Second Coming of the Savior, let us imagine in our mind's eye the scene in heaven, at the consummation of all things, when—we hope—all creatures are reconciled to one another and to their Maker, when God's will is done everywhere, on earth as in heaven. Let us envision the scene where every creature of every kind, myriads upon myriads, stands before the throne, arms linked and faces beaming, singing as with a single voice: "Yea, amen! Let all adore thee, high on thine eternal throne; Savior, take the power and glory; claim the kingdom for thine own: Alleluia! Alleluia! Thou shalt reign, and thou alone!"

## PRAYER

Come, Lord Jesus! Although we cannot know when or in what guise you shall come, we anticipate the day of your return to reign over us. "Cause of endless exultation, with what rapture shall we gaze upon your glorious scars!" And may the hearts of those who weep at your appearing be turned to you as well and their wailing turned to shouts of acclamation.

For now, Lord Jesus, we prepare for your coming by doing as you did. Move us to welcome the stranger, clothe the naked, and visit the sick and those in prison, that at your coming we will hear you say to us, "Come, O blessed of my Father, inherit the kingdom prepared for you from the foundation of the world." Amen. Come, Lord Jesus!

Amen.

# 25

## LOVE DIVINE,
## ALL LOVES EXCELLING

Charles Wesley (1707-1788)                    Suggested tune: *Blaenwern*

*Love divine, all loves excelling, joy of heaven, to earth come down,*
*fix in us thy humble dwelling, all thy faithful mercies crown.*
*Jesus, thou art all compassion, pure, unbounded love thou art;*
*visit us with thy salvation, enter every trembling heart.*

*Come, almighty to deliver, let us all thy life receive;*
*suddenly return, and never, nevermore thy temples leave.*
*Thee we would be always blessing, serve thee as thy hosts above,*
*pray, and praise thee without ceasing, glory in thy perfect love.*

*Breathe, O breathe thy loving Spirit into every troubled breast!*
*Let us all in thee inherit; let us find thy promised rest.*
*Take away the power of sinning; Alpha and Omega be;*
*end of faith as its beginning, set our hearts at liberty.*

*Finish then thy new creation; pure and spotless let us be;*
*let us see thy great salvation perfectly restored in thee,*
*changed from glory into glory, till in heaven we take our place,*
*till we cast our crowns before thee, lost in wonder, love, and praise.*

This hymn is addressed to Christ and asks that he enter and sanctify the singer's life. Charles Wesley and his brother John did not agree with the heavy emphasis on sin and depravity popular among the Puritans but thought that with the gift of divine grace, holiness of life could at least be aimed at and hoped for. Some hymnal editors omit the third stanza, thinking that it asks for the cancelling of human free will, a meaning Charles Wesley would never have intended (as indicated by the final line of the stanza). This text has been set to several fine tunes. My favorite is *Blaenwern*, written by William Penfro Rowlands, a Welsh composer, in 1905. I have heard this hymn sung to *Blaenwern* in England, Wales, and Nigeria but never in America.

*Love divine, all loves excelling, joy of heaven, to earth come down,*
*fix in us thy humble dwelling, all thy faithful mercies crown.*
*Jesus, thou art all compassion, pure, unbounded love thou art;*
*visit us with thy salvation, enter every trembling heart.*

We now know that the universe is not a three-storied construction with an "up" and a "down." Some people abandon the spatial imagery of the Bible and the classical Christian creeds that suggest God "comes down" and Jesus "ascended" into heaven, thinking such imagery renders the Christian gospel absurd.

The Christian gospel may indeed be absurd but not because of the spatial imagery we use to express it. God is not above doing absurd things. But just what is God doing?

Along with Jews, Muslims, and most people throughout history, Christians believe in a reality beyond or outside the material world of our senses. Theologians call this reality the "transcendent" or the "supernatural" (see Hymn #19). We get intimations of the transcendent in various ways, but for Christians, the definitive disclosure of it comes in the person of Jesus Christ. What we see in Jesus is the transcendent God, "pure, unbounded love," expressed in human form. We also experience this love in our lives today.

But Jesus shows us the honor of waiting for an invitation from us. That's what this hymn does—it invites Jesus to come to us, asking that "love divine, all loves excelling, joy of heaven, to earth come down."

But must we use expressions like "come down?" Well, what other language would you use? I used the words beyond and outside—two other spatial terms—a few sentences back. Spatial imagery is no worse than any other. All human language is inadequate to express who God is and what God is doing, and if it seems absurd that God would stoop (another spatial term) to interact with mere human beings, then so be it. God is not above (yet another spatial term) doing absurd things.

So come down, descend to us, holy Jesus, love divine. "Visit us with thy salvation." Our hearts are open to receive you and tremble to anticipate your arrival.

*Come, almighty to deliver, let us all thy life receive;*
*suddenly return, and never, nevermore thy temples leave.*
*Thee we would be always blessing, serve thee as thy hosts above,*
*pray, and praise thee without ceasing, glory in thy perfect love.*

We have known you in times past, O love divine, for you offer to come down to us not sporadically but continually. You are an ever-flowing spring.

But we have turned away from you. Temples we have been, but to other gods and other loves, entertaining tawdry guests in our rooms, with our doors closed and locked to you. "Suddenly return," O love divine; startle us, for it seems we pay no heed to your gentler advances. Suddenly return so that we cannot help but notice and receive you. Break down our doors. Enter to sweep clean our floors, repair our broken fixtures, refinish our dull surfaces, repaint our mildewed walls, and brighten every corner of every room. Make us temples fit for your habitation. "Come, almighty to deliver, let us all thy life receive," and when that is done, then "never, nevermore thy temples leave." We would be always blessing you, serving you "as thy hosts above." We would pray and praise you "without ceasing."

Or at least we think we would. We're learning about your blessing, your service, your glory, and your love, but we're easily distracted, slow students who forget today what we learned yesterday. Bear with us, O love divine.

*Breathe, O breathe thy loving Spirit into every troubled breast!*
*Let us all in thee inherit; let us find thy promised rest.*
*Take away the power of sinning; Alpha and Omega be;*
*end of faith as its beginning, set our hearts at liberty.*

We invite you, O love divine, to "breathe thy loving Spirit into every troubled breast"—but maybe we don't really mean it. We're not sure we truly want you to come down to us.

You may have to force your way in, battering the door until it can no longer keep you out. If our invitation to you is tepid, insincere, or conditional, then do what you must do to breathe your loving Spirit into us. Make it impossible for us to resist you. Then give to us your "promised rest," the rest that comes from our having been transformed into your willing and faithful servants. Both Alpha and Omega be, both the originator and the goal of our faith.

We also ask you, O love divine, to remove certain powers from us. In fact, we beg you to remove them. The misuse of the powers you have given us has often landed us where we didn't want to be. Why should we want an array of choices when many of those choices lead to briars, fetid swamps, and barren deserts? We would happily relinquish the power to make terrible choices. Limit our choices; "take away the power of sinning."

Well, actually, we're not sure about that, either. We rather like the power of sinning. What you have already done in us, O love divine, we accept, but we haven't always liked the way you did it. Your cleansing agents rub hard and penetrate deep. Sometimes they remove what we'd rather hold onto. We are glad we're less smudged than we once were, but we're comfortable with our remaining smudges and not eager to see them washed away. They seem fairly harmless to us, and they do give us pleasure.

*Finish then thy new creation; pure and spotless let us be;*
*let us see thy great salvation perfectly restored in thee,*
*changed from glory into glory, till in heaven we take our place,*
*till we cast our crowns before thee, lost in wonder, love, and praise.*

We do and we don't want to be made "pure and spotless." We both long for you and shrink from you. We pray for purity and spotlessness with half our heart, but the other half does not join this prayer. We can't change that; it is who we are. But you can change it, O love divine. You can finish what you have begun in us, the half-done remaking of ourselves that we halfway want to see carried through. Listen to what within us is surrendered to you; and what is not, bring into submission by whatever means you choose. Unify our conflicted thoughts and longings. Make us to be of one heart, one mind, and one will, one complete self fully surrendered to you. "Let us see thy great salvation"—let us see ourselves— "perfectly restored in thee."

Change us from this glory into another, and from that glory into another, and then another and another (2 Corinthians 3:18). Let us move from glory to glory "till in heaven we take our place," and then let us move further and deeper, still from glory to glory, as you draw us more and more into your presence. Deeper and deeper, nearer and nearer, but never arriving, for how could such as we ever arrive at you? You are not our destination, O love divine, but our eternal goal, always around us and within us, yet always beyond us, always beckoning.

When "in heaven we take our place," we shall "cast our crowns before thee," around that crystal sea, "lost in wonder, love, and praise." What use have we for these silly crowns, anyway? Do we think we rule someone, something, somewhere? These crowns are the fanciful products of our vain imaginations. They have grown tarnished and heavy, burdens weighing us down but which we have been loath to drop. In heaven, O love divine, we shall cast our crowns before thee. But why in heaven and not on earth? Why not here? Why not today, why not every day, lost in wonder, love, and praise? Claim what is your own, O love divine, all loves excelling. "Joy of heaven, to earth come down!"

##  PRAYER

Fill our hearts, our minds, our wills, our memories, O love divine. Then our service to you will be joyful, free, and whole; we will glory in you because we will have become indistinguishable from you. And don't wait for heaven. Let it begin here, today.

*Amen.*

# 26

## MAKE ME A CAPTIVE, LORD

George Matheson (1842-1906)                    Suggested tune: *Llanllyfni*

*Make me a captive, Lord, and then I shall be free;*
*force me to render up my sword, and I shall conqueror be.*
*I sink in life's alarms when by myself I stand;*
*imprison me within thine arms, and strong shall be my hand.*

*My heart is weak and poor until it master find;*
*it has no spring of action sure; it varies with the wind.*
*It cannot freely move till thou hast wrought its chain;*
*enslave it with thy matchless love, and deathless it shall reign.*

*My will is not my own till thou hast made it thine;*
*if I would reach a monarch's throne, I must my crown resign.*
*I only stand unbent amid the clashing strife,*
*when on thy bosom I have leant, and found in thee my life.*

This hymn revolves around the paradox of 2 Corinthians
12:9-10: "He said to me, 'My grace is sufficient for you, for
power is made perfect in weakness.' So, I will boast all the
more gladly of my weaknesses, so that the power of Christ
may dwell in me. Therefore I am content with weaknesses,
insults, hardships, persecutions, and calamities for the

sake of Christ; for whenever I am weak, then I am strong."
George Matheson was a respected Presbyterian preacher
and author (see Hymn #32). *Llanllyfni* was composed by the
nineteenth-century Welsh composer John Jones.

*Make me a captive, Lord, and then I shall be free;*
*force me to render up my sword, and I shall conqueror be.*
*I sink in life's alarms when by myself I stand;*
*imprison me within thine arms, and strong shall be my hand.*

The paradox of strength in weakness is expressed in images
that work within this hymn's framework but would be
jarring in any other context. The singer asks to be captured,
imprisoned, and (in the next stanza) chained and enslaved—
hardly a request most people would make.

We're talking about the conflict in the human soul between
willfulness and surrender. The hymn recognizes that spiritual
vitality comes only from surrendering our souls to God but
also that our resistance to that surrender can be dogged.

For years I tried to take charge, to wield my sword, without
having first surrendered and submitted. I was wielding my
sword for the kingdom of God (or so I thought), but it didn't
work. The harder I strived, the more anxious, frightened,
and cynical I became. Finally, excessive drink and exhaustion
drove me to my knees. When after some years I surrendered
to the God I had ostensibly served, I felt liberated. I no
longer had to be right, set the agenda, and get my way. It

was as if a burden had been lifted from my shoulders, as if the sun had emerged after a prolonged darkness, as if tense muscles had suddenly relaxed. Things went more smoothly for me after that—and I achieved more of my goals. Why had I waited so long to put into practice what I had for years been preaching to others?

> My heart is weak and poor until it master find;
> it has no spring of action sure; it varies with the wind.
> It cannot freely move till thou hast wrought its chain;
> enslave it with thy matchless love, and deathless it shall reign.

The question of human free will is a knotty one. Sigmund Freud, the founder of psychoanalysis, discovered the unconscious part of our minds that exerts a huge and invisible influence over what we do. Then there are attitudes picked up in childhood, genetic factors, religious and political convictions, and addictions of various kinds. We are not as free as we think; everyone is bound in ways both seen and unseen.

Yet we do have choices, and our choices are real. They are neither predetermined nor entirely predictable. Some people make a decision that flies in the face of everything their past would suggest. People can decide to change; we can choose to surrender or not, and we can choose to whom or what we surrender. I was not, for example, bound to enter alcoholism recovery. Some alcoholics make that decision, but many do not; every addict freely chooses to get well or to die of his addiction.

To submit to God (or the "Higher Power," in recovery lingo) is a free choice. For most of us, the choice must be renewed daily. When we willingly allow ourselves to be bound by our loving

God rather than by something else, God obliges us by directing and ruling our lives. His "service is perfect freedom."

> *My will is not my own till thou hast made it thine;*
> *if I would reach a monarch's throne, I must my crown resign.*
> *I only stand unbent amid the clashing strife,*
> *when on thy bosom I have leant, and found in thee my life.*

It's a matter of the will. Most people don't know what's most important to them. I was recently told of a group of people asked to identify the seven things most important to them and to write each on a slip of paper. Then they were asked to let go of one slip of paper and retain just six things. Then they were asked to let another paper go, and then another, until they were left with just one slip of paper. The exercise was revealing and, for many, troubling, because they hadn't known until that moment what was most important to them and they didn't always like what they discovered about themselves.

To submit to God may require a radical reorienting of our priorities and may create tension and conflict with those closest to us. Submission is a free decision, an act of the will that activates the paradox of which this hymn is a forceful expression: to be victorious and free is to have completely surrendered.

## ⸙ PRAYER ⸙

Dear God, I must have been hard to endure as a young man. I was so full of myself! You surely realized (and I hope the people around me realized) that my self-assured exuberance would pass. I didn't know who I was in those days.

I still don't know who I am. I hope I am your man these days, but I am not sure. I am no longer sure of anything. I enjoy a pleasant life, but I don't know that it's a faithful life. I don't even know what a faithful life is. But I hope that I please you, my God, and that you will receive me for my hope.

I have often surrendered to you in the past, or thought I did, like when at the age of twelve I answered the altar call at a Billy Graham crusade, my first intentional Christian commitment, and years later when I took a position in an obscure backwater, turning my back on career advancement. But my most dramatic surrender, no doubt, was my entry into alcoholism recovery in 1983 at the age of thirty-eight. Thank you for coming to me when I called to you, gracious God, and for removing the desire to drink from me. The ensuing years have been vastly happier and more productive than those before my recovery. But have they been more faithful? Have my acts of surrender been the real thing? Or have I been playing games with myself, dancing to my own beat while pretending to dance to yours? I sometimes think my entire life as a Christian, and especially as a Christian priest, has been one long, uninterrupted pretense.

And so yet again I come to surrender to you. I submit all things to you. Do with me as you will. Let me work or let me be idle. Let me be praised or let me be scorned. Give me everything or give me nothing. These are scary words, dear God, and I am not sure I really mean them, so capture and subdue me until these words become truly mine. Break me if I need breaking, then melt me and mold me into the vessel of your choosing, and then fill me with yourself. Take my freedom and direct me. Shape my will to your glory. You are all I need or want, dear Lord. Make my surrender complete, for then I shall be truly free.

*Amen.*

# 27

# MORNING HAS BROKEN

Eleanor Farjeon (1881-1965)                    Suggested tune: *Bunessan*

*Morning has broken like the first morning;*
*blackbird has spoken like the first bird.*
*Praise for the singing, praise for the morning,*
*praise for them springing fresh from the Word.*

*Sweet the rain's new fall, sunlit from heaven,*
*like the first dewfall on the first grass.*
*Praise for the sweetness of the wet garden,*
*sprung in completeness where his feet pass.*

*Mine is the sunlight, mine is the morning,*
*born of the one light Eden saw play.*
*Praise with elation, praise every morning,*
*God's recreation of the new day.*

The Gaelic folk tune *Bunessan* came first. Then Percy
Dearmer commissioned poet Eleanor Farjeon, known for
writing magical tales for children, to write a text to be sung
to the tune for *Songs of Praise*, an English hymnal published
in 1931 and edited by Dearmer. The hymn became popular in
America when sung by folk singer Cat Stevens in the 1970s.
Since then, it has appeared in numerous hymnals.

*Morning has broken like the first morning;*
*blackbird has spoken like the first bird.*
*Praise for the singing, praise for the morning,*
*praise for them springing fresh from the Word.*

As I grow older, my sleep pattern—if you can call it a pattern—
has become unpredictable. Sometimes, for no apparent
reason, I awaken well before sunrise, wide-eyed and pumped
for the day. When that happens, I often get up, dress, step out
onto my porch, and sit down to pray. Those early mornings on
the porch, begun in darkness, continuing as the light gradually
filters through the trees, and ending in the fullness of the
day, are among my favorite moments. Some of this book was
written during those early mornings on the porch. I especially
enjoy rising before the birds (that's early!) and listening for the
first birdsong breaking the silence of night. Within moments, a
chorus of birds joins in the anthem.

Of course I know that nature isn't always beautiful; it can be
cruel. And I know that people can be cruel to one another. I
try not to ignore the needs and sufferings of others and to do
my part. But those precious moments alone with God at dawn,
surrounded by the trees and the birds, are not a denial of the
world's pain. Rather, they are occasions for quiet thanksgiving,
for refreshment, for recharging my spiritual batteries, for
recalling that God rules and that God rules well, the headlines
and newscasts notwithstanding. Jesus often retreated to the
mountains for time alone. If he sang during his mountain
retreats, I expect it was a song much like this one.

*Sweet the rain's new fall, sunlit from heaven,*
*like the first dewfall on the first grass.*
*Praise for the sweetness of the wet garden,*
*sprung in completeness where his feet pass.*

The Alabama Gulf Coast receives more rainfall each year
than any other spot in the forty-eight contiguous states
(Hilo, Hawaii, is the only place in the U.S. receiving more).
That means that when I'm sitting on my porch, rain is often
falling in the yard a few feet from me. I like to close my eyes
and listen to the faint clicking sound as the raindrops strike
the magnolia leaves. I imagine the rain sifting down into the
ground, loosening it and preparing it to produce an array of
green things. One of my favorite Bible verses comes to mind:
"You sent a gracious rain, O God, upon your inheritance;
you refreshed the land when it was weary" (Psalm 68:9).
Sometimes I drift back to sleep on the porch as I listen to the
falling rain.

Then there is the sunlight. Spring temperatures begin to
arrive in south Alabama in late February. The air will still be
crisp some days, but the warm sun will be shining brightly.
That's when I slip down to Mobile Bay, unfold my hammock
chair onto the sand, and nap for an hour in my windbreaker
as the sunbeams warm my cheeks and I listen to the sea gulls
and the waves breaking on the beach.

It's easy to praise God at moments like these and to picture
in my mind "the sweetness of the wet garden, sprung in
completeness where his feet pass." God is many things, most
of them beyond our understanding, but the gentle rain and
the warm sunlight give us hints of God's life-generating
energy and sublime beauty.

*Mine is the sunlight, mine is the morning,*
*born of the one light Eden saw play.*
*Praise with elation, praise every morning,*
*God's recreation of the new day.*

I like the word recreation in the final line of this hymn. It suggests something about the Creation—with a capital C, meaning God's Creation of the universe—that I am just now beginning to grasp. For years I thought of the Creation as something that had happened a long time ago—six thousand years ago according to biblical literalists, 13.8 billion years ago according to astrophysicists. Either way, Creation was in the past. I liked the image of a watch being wound up: God had wound up the universe and set it running a long time ago. The universe had been ticking away ever since.

But I now see the Creation not as something God did way back then, but as something God is doing right now, something God is always doing. God continually empowers all things to exist, rather as the light in a motion picture projector shines through the lens to project the figures onto the screen. Those figures walk and talk and do things, giving the impression that they are self-sufficient, independent entities with minds and wills of their own. But they are mere creatures of the light in the projector. Turn that light off and *Poof!* The figures on the screen don't just cease to move—they cease to exist.

We depend on God in something like the same way, moment to moment. God "recreates" us every second of our lives. His loving attention to us is continual and uninterrupted. "Praise with elation, praise every morning, God's recreation of the new day."

## PRAYER

When I sit quietly, looking into the woods and listening to the birds, enjoying the cool breeze as summer arrives or wrapped in a soft blanket in the coolness of the south Alabama winter, everything feels right, dear Lord. If there are conflicts and tragedies, they don't impinge on me during those moments. Is that what Eden was like? Do you give me those moments to remind me of what you intended for your world and what will be again when all things find their consummation and bliss in you? Are those moments a taste of heaven on earth?

Thank you for such moments, precious Lord. May I never take them for granted. I accept them for what they are: refreshing interludes between busier, more productive moments. Those moments are important, too, and I am grateful for them, for things to do and deadlines to meet. But it's these interlude moments, when I can breathe the freshness of your Creation deep into my lungs, that I most treasure. They make me glad to be alive and glad to be alive in this world. Thank you, Lord.

*Amen.*

# 28

# O FOR A THOUSAND TONGUES TO SING

Charles Wesley (1707-1788)                    Suggested tune: *Azmon*

O for a thousand tongues to sing my great Redeemer's praise,
the glories of my God and King, the triumphs of his grace!

My gracious Master and my God, assist me to proclaim,
and spread through all the earth abroad the honors of thy name.

Jesus! the name that charms our fears, that bids our sorrows cease:
'tis music in the sinner's ears, 'tis life, and health, and peace.

He speaks, and, listening to his voice, new life the dead receive,
the mournful, broken hearts rejoice, the humble poor believe.

Hear him, ye deaf; ye speechless ones, your loosened tongues
      employ;
ye blind, behold your Savior come, and leap, ye lame, for joy.

Glory to God, and praise and love be now and ever given,
by saints below and saints above, the church in earth and heaven.

This hymn was written in 1739 for the first anniversary of the author's conversion. As with Charles Wesley's hymns generally (four are discussed in these pages), this one celebrates the grace and love of God to undeserving sinners. These six stanzas are drawn from the eighteen stanzas of Wesley's original. Stanza seven in Wesley's text serves here as the opening stanza, as it does today the world over. In Methodist hymnals worldwide, this hymn is usually Hymn #1. *Azmon* was written in 1828 by the German composer Carl Gotthilf Gläser.

---

*O for a thousand tongues to sing my great Redeemer's praise,*
*the glories of my God and King, the triumphs of his grace!*

Charles Wesley must have had at least a thousand tongues to sing his great Redeemer's praise, for he wrote roughly 9,000 hymns, many of them with twenty or more stanzas. That's one hymn every three days for sixty years. Four hundred or so of Wesley's hymns are still sung somewhere in the world today. He wrote hymns everywhere. Once, after composing a hymn in his mind while riding his horse, he stopped, dismounted, and ran into a friend's house shouting, "Pen and paper! Pen and paper!" Charles Wesley is the English language's greatest hymnist.

Wesley's hymns broke new ground. The Church of England had frowned on "enthusiasm" and sang only biblical and liturgical texts, often listlessly. Wesley's hymns, however, are intensely personal, sprinkled with phrases like "enable me to stand," "keep me ever thine," "I seek to touch my Lord," and "the joy prepared for me." This gives his hymns a robust, warm, intimate quality. Immediately popular in England's Methodist chapels, Wesley's hymns did not find favor among Anglicans until a century later. They are sung today by Christians of diverse denominations.

I don't write hymns, but if I did, I'd aspire to write like Charles Wesley.

*My gracious Master and my God, assist me to proclaim,*
*and spread through all the earth abroad the honors of thy name.*

Even with a thousand tongues, I'm not sure I could adequately proclaim my great Redeemer's praise to the family next door, much less to people from far away with experiences and understandings very different from mine. How can someone who understands as little as I do spread anything "through all the earth abroad?"

When opportunities to proclaim the gospel have come to me, I have often stumbled over my words. That awkwardness was all the more evident a few years ago when I taught spirituality and church history in Nigeria. My students were fervent Christians, but they asked questions unlike those my American students typically ask, and I had no ready answers.

I quickly learned in Nigeria not to pretend that I knew answers to questions when I didn't. I also learned that the best proclamation is with generous, loving deeds. After all, when God chose to reveal himself in the most definitive way, he didn't send a book with a lot of words. He came in person to show us what love looks like. He healed the sick,

wept with the grieving, forgave the sinful, welcomed the
outcast. Some of Jesus' words were written down and words
are important, but if words were all we had of Jesus, he would
be remembered as a mere prophet. His words have power
because Jesus did what he did and was who he was. That's true
for us as well: It's what we do and who we are that proclaims
the message, and when we feel inadequate, God will "assist"
us to proclaim it.

*Jesus! the name that charms our fears, that bids our sorrows cease:
'tis music in the sinner's ears, 'tis life, and health, and peace.*

"At the name of Jesus every knee should bend," Saint Paul
wrote to the Philippians (2:10). There is a long tradition of
honoring the name of Jesus, dating back at least to Bernard
of Clairvaux in the twelfth century, and many have derived
strength from meditating on the divine name. But the
syllables and letters of a name, even Jesus' name, carry no
more power in themselves than other syllables and letters. A
name gets its power because it points to a person. That's why
schoolyard taunts about a child's name can hurt so deeply.

It's Jesus himself, not his name only, who "charms our fears
and bids our sorrows cease." He doesn't do it by showing
us that our fears and sorrows are unfounded. Tragic events
occur. Fear will not prevent them, and it's sometimes
understandable, even wise to be afraid. Moreover, sorrow
for the loss of a loved one is a natural expression of our
love. Jesus himself wept at the tomb of his friend Lazarus.
No, Jesus charms our fears and bids our sorrows cease by
searching us out in the fearful and sorrowful places where
we sit trembling and weeping. Jesus has in fact visited those

places many times and knows them intimately. We never suffer alone.

Philip Yancey, a contemporary Christian writer, tells of an old rabbinic saying that "Where the Messiah is, there is no misery." Jesus, Yancey says, has turned that saying upside down so that Christians can say, "Where misery is, there is the Messiah." Our fears are finally charmed and our sorrows cease because Jesus holds us in his arms and mingles his tears with our own.

*He speaks, and, listening to his voice, new life the dead receive, the mournful, broken hearts rejoice, the humble poor believe.*

I once went through several years of anger, confusion, and exhaustion. I felt demoralized, misunderstood, broken, and estranged from family and friends. The faith I had once cherished seemed a distant memory. I identified with Lazarus in the dark tomb (John 11). Perhaps I was spiritually dead, my soul starting to decay. Looking back now, I recognize that I was paralyzed by self-pity, self-love, and self-will. The idolatry of self was consuming me. It's not surprising that my faith had begun to fray.

For months I prayed to the God in whom I no longer believed because that's all I knew to do, but my confusion was unrelieved. Then one day I heard a faint voice calling in my mind: "Lazarus, come out!" Recognizing it as a voice I had heard before, I rallied my rotting limbs, lurched to my feet, and groped through the darkness toward that voice. Then I heard the voice say, "Unbind him! Let him go!"

That was several decades ago. It was the beginning of

resurrection for me. I had to put my swollen pride behind and trust Christ as I had never done before. Apparently, I had been unwilling to trust Christ until the pain became acute. Perhaps it's always like that. A new life, brighter than any I had known before, began to dawn for me. I believe it had been prepared for me and that its Author had been patiently waiting for me to claim it.

I know what this stanza is about. It's about me. It may be about every Christian.

> Hear him, ye deaf; ye speechless ones, your loosened tongues
>     employ;
> ye blind, behold your Savior come, and leap, ye lame, for joy.

In the summer of 1975, at the age of thirty-one, I felt a familiar pain in my side. A similar pain had laid me low three times in the previous four years, so I knew what it was: My left kidney was infected, again. Antibiotics had cured me before, but I'd had enough of kidney infections, so I consulted a urologist. He recommended the removal of my kidney.

Never having had major surgery before, I was frightened. For the first time, I seriously pondered my mortality. My surgeon knew this; we discussed it. But when the operation was over, he told me he had rarely operated on a patient who seemed as calm going into surgery as I had been. He asked what had happened to curtail my fear.

"In my mind, I sang a stanza of a familiar hymn over and over," I told him. This was the stanza. I must have sung it in my mind thirty times before drifting off under the anesthesia. Images of Christ healing the deaf, the dumb, the blind, and the lame filled my imagination, and I began to feel that come what may, all would be well.

I don't want to make too much of that experience. Singing and praying guarantee nothing, but this stanza of this hymn calmed my mind at a critical, risky moment. I believe my calm spirit contributed to the success of the surgery. My surgeon said as much afterward.

> *Glory to God, and praise and love be now and ever given,*
> *by saints below and saints above, the church in earth and heaven.*

We sing to glorify God, and not just we, but myriads of creatures "now and ever." If modern physicists are right, even the phrase "now and ever" is too limited, for creatures outside of time, unknown and unknowable to us, may be glorifying God in their own ways. There may also be creatures outside our spatial universe who glorify God in their own ways. The words "saints below and saints above, the church in earth and heaven" refer to "places" where even the word place may have no meaning. They too join their voices with ours. It is the chorus of eternity.

## PRAYER

I have but one tongue to sing your praise, Lord Jesus, and I hesitate to use it because in praising you for one blessing, I neglect numberless others. My tongue can express only what my mind contains, and no thought of mine can adequately declare your glory. All the words I have sung or ever shall sing are as nothing before you. And yet I cannot remain silent.

I sing, then, not merely to praise you, Jesus, but to express my joy, to call to mind yet again the blessings you have showered upon me and the glimpses of glory you have disclosed to me. Join my voice to those of the pilgrims who travel the King's highway alongside me, the great saints who have traveled that way in the past, and the angels and archangels whose "Holy, holy, holy" echoes around your heavenly throne.

And finally, Lord Jesus, may my songs of praise express not only the devotion of my heart but also the life I live. May my every thought, word, and deed be an act of praise. So enter and fill me, Lord, that in my song, it is you yourself who sing. May my voice become your voice.

*Amen.*

# 29

# O JESUS, I HAVE PROMISED

John Ernest Bode (1816-1874)                    Suggested tune: *Llanfyllin*

*O Jesus, I have promised to serve thee to the end;*
*be thou forever near me, my Master and my friend.*
*I shall not fear the battle, if thou art by my side,*
*nor wander from the pathway, if thou wilt be my guide.*

*O let me feel thee near me; the world is ever near;*
*I see the sights that dazzle, the tempting sounds I hear.*
*My foes are ever near me, around me and within;*
*but, Jesus, draw thou nearer, and shield my soul from sin.*

*O let me hear thee speaking in accents clear and still,*
*above the storms of passion, the murmurs of self-will.*
*O speak to reassure me, to hasten or control;*
*O speak, and make me listen, thou guardian of my soul.*

*O Jesus, thou hast promised to all who follow thee,*
*that where thou art in glory there shalt thy servant be;*
*and Jesus, I have promised to serve thee to the end;*
*O give me grace to follow, my Master and my friend.*

*O let me see thy footprints and in them plant my own;*
*my hope to follow duly, is in thy strength alone;*
*O guide me, call me, draw me, uphold me to the end;*
*and then in heav'n receive me, my Savior and my friend.*

John Ernest Bode, a priest of the Church of England, wrote
this hymn for three of his children on their confirmation
day in 1866. It contains "all the important truths I want you
to remember when you are fully confirmed," he told them.
*Llanfyllin* is a traditional Welsh tune.

*O Jesus, I have promised to serve thee to the end;*
*be thou forever near me, my Master and my friend.*
*I shall not fear the battle, if thou art by my side,*
*nor wander from the pathway, if thou wilt be my guide.*

"To the end" sounds like a long time. Yes, I have promised
to serve Jesus to the end, and so far, I have kept my promise,
intermittently, more or less. I'm not sure about tomorrow.

Part of my problem is the way Jesus is often portrayed—
ethereal, wispy, bland, like vanilla pudding or beige
wallpaper or a doily. I can't identify with that. At other times
Jesus is portrayed seated high on his heavenly throne, *Rex
tremendae majestatis.* That might frighten me into keeping
my promise, but my heart wouldn't be in it. And sometimes
Jesus is portrayed as a pinched, vinegary spoilsport.

Jesus, if I am to serve you to the end, I want to know you as a
real flesh-and-blood person like me, as someone who laughs
and cries, grows tired and needs a break, misunderstands and
is misunderstood, gets impatient and befuddled, and cracks
jokes that occasionally fall flat.

You are also "my Master" (or at least I've promised to accept you as Master), but today I want you to be my friend, somebody I can hang out with, doing nothing in particular, just enjoying your company. If I am to keep my promise to serve you to the end, I want you to be more than my Master.

Please, Jesus, be "my Master and my friend," and let's start with friend. I'm going to the ballgame this evening. Want to come along?

> O let me feel thee near me; the world is ever near;
> I see the sights that dazzle, the tempting sounds I hear.
> My foes are ever near me, around me and within;
> but, Jesus, draw thou nearer, and shield my soul from sin.

I'm sure Jesus saw "the sights that dazzle" and heard "the tempting sounds" in his day. With Hollywood, Madison Avenue, and the internet, today's sights and sounds may be more dazzling and tempting than those Jesus knew, but the message surely hasn't changed: Go for what feels good, entertain yourself, get ahead, because it's all about you and you deserve it.

Jesus, you ignored those sights and sounds. You knew what mattered and kept it in view, or if you didn't, you quickly saw your error and corrected your course. I want to do that too. I want to be like you, Jesus, but I'm not like you. I'm either unable or unwilling. When I try to be like you, sooner or later I slip and fall, every time. So I need you to be near me, and more than that, I need to feel you near me, to know you're near me. Sometimes I don't feel your presence, Jesus. Sometimes I feel abandoned, lost, out there all by myself.

*O let me hear thee speaking in accents clear and still,*
*above the storms of passion, the murmurs of self-will.*
*O speak to reassure me, to hasten or control;*
*O speak, and make me listen, thou guardian of my soul.*

Jesus, you have been speaking for millennia in various ways, but you don't always speak "in accents clear and still." Sometimes you speak ambiguously and obscurely, giving mere hints of what you mean to say, and sometimes one hint seems to contradict another. The meaning of some of your parables is opaque. Apparently, you want me to wrestle with what you're saying. And then there are those "storms of passion" and "murmurs of self-will" that drown out your voice even when it is clear and still. Jesus, speak plainly!

*"You're quite a talker yourself, you know. Every time I try to 'reassure' you, to 'hasten or control,' you seem to be talking. Blah, blah, blah! No wonder you don't get what I'm saying. And you're the one who generates those storms of passion and murmurs of self-will. I might as well be addressing a concrete block.*

*"Yes, I like for you to wrestle with what I say, because wrestling strengthens the sinews of your soul. If I made everything obvious, you'd never have to think. That's why I let you keep talking and don't blow you over with a noise you couldn't ignore. You've asked me to make you listen, but I won't do it. I'd rather wait for you to come around on your own. But the fact that you want me to make you listen is a good sign. You're getting there."*

*O Jesus, thou hast promised to all who follow thee,*
*that where thou art in glory there shalt thy servant be;*

*and Jesus, I have promised to serve thee to the end;*
*O give me grace to follow, my Master and my friend.*

I want to be with you, Jesus, to be one of your friends, but
I'm not sure I'm ready for your glory. What is your glory
exactly? I'm thinking it's you, the second person of the holy
and undivided Trinity, God from God, Light from Light,
seated at the right hand of the Father, radiating power and
energy. Are we talking in heaven, here on earth, or both? And
couldn't your glory burn me or blind me? How about we meet
someplace where your glory is turned down to low or medium?

*"You're already with me in my glory. You see my glory when*
*you look into the faces of your children, your friends, your*
*colleagues at work—and your enemies and detractors (you need*
*to practice seeing my glory in them). My glory is everywhere, in*
*every created thing, in every creature I make and love. Look in*
*the mirror; you'll see my glory there, too. You are my glory. I*
*will give you, as you have asked, grace to follow and serve me to*
*the end, but you must understand that you are already there."*

*O let me see thy footprints and in them plant my own;*
*my hope to follow duly, is in thy strength alone;*
*O guide me, call me, draw me, uphold me to the end;*
*and then in heav'n receive me, my Savior and my friend.*

To follow in your footprints, Jesus, I must see them. I know
I can see them if I really want to see them; what obscures
them is of my own making. I would remove those blinders,
but I can only do it "in thy strength alone." My own resolve
is insufficient; Jesus, you must enable me to follow you. "My
hope to follow duly, is in thy strength alone."

## PRAYER

"O guide me, call me, draw me, uphold me to the end," Lord Jesus. Guide me because I cannot discern the right path on my own. Call me because I need to hear your voice. Draw me to you like filings to a magnet. Uphold me lest I fall. If you will not compel me to follow, then so overwhelm me that other paths lose their luster. Ravish my soul, Lord Jesus, that I may so love you that I desire nothing more than to be with you, all other longings encompassed in my longing for you. "And then in heav'n receive me, my Savior and my friend."

*Amen.*

# 30

# O LITTLE TOWN OF BETHLEHEM

Phillips Brooks (1835-1893)                    Suggested tune: *St. Louis*

*O little town of Bethlehem, how still we see thee lie!*
*Above thy deep and dreamless sleep the silent stars go by;*
*yet in thy dark streets shineth the everlasting light;*
*the hopes and dreams of all the years are met in thee tonight.*

*For Christ is born of Mary; and gathered all above,*
*while mortals sleep, the angels keep their watch of wondering love.*
*O morning stars, together proclaim the holy birth!*
*and praises sing to God the King, and peace to all the earth.*

*How silently, how silently, the wondrous gift is given!*
*So God imparts to human hearts the blessing of his heaven.*
*No ear may hear his coming, but in this world of sin,*
*where meek souls will receive him, still the dear Christ enters in.*

*Where children pure and happy pray to the blessed child,*
*where misery cries out to thee, son of the mother mild;*
*where charity stands watching and faith holds wide the door,*
*the dark night wakes, the glory breaks, and Christmas comes*
        *once more.*

*O holy child of Bethlehem, descend to us, we pray;*
*cast out our sin and enter in, be born in us today.*
*We hear the Christmas angels the great glad tidings tell;*
*O come to us, abide with us, our Lord Emmanuel!*

Inspired by spending Christmas Eve 1865 in Bethlehem, Phillips Brooks, rector of Holy Trinity Episcopal Church in Philadelphia at the time, wrote this hymn in 1868. *St. Louis* was composed for it by Brooks's organist, Lewis H. Redner.

*O little town of Bethlehem, how still we see thee lie!*
*Above thy deep and dreamless sleep the silent stars go by;*
*yet in thy dark streets shineth the everlasting light;*
*the hopes and dreams of all the years are met in thee tonight.*

Bethlehem? Have you ever been there? It's part of the disputed West Bank and a place where Christians of various hues bicker and compete at the presumed birthplace of their Savior. It's not much of a place. In biblical times, Bethlehem was the boyhood home of David, Israel's greatest king, its only claim to fame. It wasn't much a place then either.

The Son of God could have been born in Rome or Jerusalem but chose Bethlehem for his nativity and was then reared in Nazareth, another prosaic little place. In modern terms, he passed up New York and Los Angeles in favor of a couple of villages in, say, Malawi or Paraguay. Why the little town of Bethlehem, of all places?

It could have been any of the thousands of little towns found in every nation of the world. Urbanites like to dismiss little towns as provincial, ingrown places, which they sometimes are. Little towns lie still and sleepy as "the silent stars go by." But in a little town, everyone knows everyone else and who everyone's parents and grandparents are. Everything is personal there.

And little towns aren't pretentious. Their lights don't dazzle, so that when the everlasting light appeared in the little town of Bethlehem, it was given room to grow. Maybe that's what God wanted when casting about for a place to begin his visit to his world.

> For Christ is born of Mary; and gathered all above,
> while mortals sleep, the angels keep their watch of wondering love.
> O morning stars, together proclaim the holy birth!
> and praises sing to God the King, and peace to all the earth.

When the location of the birth of the Son of God was announced, I can imagine the conversation in heaven among those angels keeping "their watch of wondering love":

- "I thought he was kidding when he first mentioned it, and when I realized he was serious, I thought he'd lost his mind."

- "I still wonder about that. It's not what you'd expect from a deity of sound mind. Granted, he's the Son of the Ancient of Days himself—or *herself* as the Ancient of Days now likes to be referred to—so of course he can do anything he chooses."

- "And the Son has long been known for his humility, but there is a difference between being humble and debasing yourself, and if you ask me, I think he's crossed that line. As a member of the royal family, he has a certain dignity to uphold."

- "I suppose that depends on what you mean by dignity. Apparently, the Son takes a different view of dignity."

- "Perhaps he's extending dignity downward by becoming one of those creatures in that obscure village on that little speck of a planet. And you realize that if the Son identifies himself with them, he is raising them to our level—or *higher!* We can hardly refuse to welcome them as equals when he has made himself their equal."

- "I suppose not, but I'm not sure I can ever fully accept it. In any case, though, we're supposed to compose and sing anthems for events of heavenly import, so we'd better get to work on some music. How about something like 'Glory to God in the highest and on earth peace, goodwill to men?'"

*How silently, how silently, the wondrous gift is given!*
*So God imparts to human hearts the blessing of his heaven.*
*No ear may hear his coming, but in this world of sin,*
*where meek souls will receive him, still the dear Christ enters in.*

The shepherds in their fields heard those angelic anthems, according to Saint Luke, but apparently no one else did, or at least no other human ear heard them. Joseph and Mary, the innkeeper, the wise men, Herod—for everyone else in the story—the birth of the Son of God seems to have occurred silently. If there was a trumpet fanfare, it made no impression. The divine birth could easily have been overlooked. Most people did in fact overlook it.

Why was the wondrous gift given in silence? Probably because it is only in silence that the gift can be received. The shepherds heard the anthems because, sitting silently in their fields, they *could* hear them. Maybe that's why, even today, so few people receive the gift. Like most people in biblical times, we fill our minds with external noises like honking horns, ringing telephones, and barking voices, and internal noises like nagging worries, obsessions, and obligations. "In this world of sin"—for that's what many of our noises are—only "meek souls" can quiet themselves to hear the anthems and receive "the blessing of his heaven," and there's not much meekness among us.

So stop and be still. Be intentional and persistent about it; it may take a while since the noises in our minds do not willingly or quickly subside. But do stop and be still, for "in this world of sin, where meek souls will receive him, still the dear Christ enters in."

> *Where children pure and happy pray to the blessed child,*
> *where misery cries out to thee, son of the mother mild;*
> *where charity stands watching and faith holds wide the door,*
> *the dark night wakes, the glory breaks, and Christmas comes*
> *once more.*

This stanza refers to four kinds of people who are present when "the dark night wakes, the glory breaks, and Christmas comes once more." They are children, the miserable, the charitable, and the faithful.

Perhaps the one thing those four groups have in common is their single-mindedness. Children have short attention spans, but they focus intently on what is at hand. Misery tends to block out other concerns. Charitable persons ignore competing priorities as they engage other people and address their needs. And to be faithful is to be present to God at all times.

For me, though, life is more complex than that. In my best moments, I may approach single-mindedness, but more often I weigh one viewpoint against another and work on several tasks at once. Multitasking is my norm. I manage my time with multiple ends in view. There's probably nothing wrong with that, and some situations require it. But it means I rarely devote my whole self to anything, and that is perhaps why it seems that for me the night rarely wakes, the glory rarely breaks, and Christmas rarely comes.

> O holy child of Bethlehem, descend to us, we pray;
> cast out our sin and enter in, be born in us today.
> We hear the Christmas angels the great glad tidings tell;
> O come to us, abide with us, our Lord Emmanuel!

Where does the holy child of Bethlehem come from? We speak of his descending to us because we sense that his true home is up there somewhere, above us, in a realm we can only think of as higher. We envision him seated for all eternity on a throne in the sky at the right hand of the Father. Is that a good way to think of the child of Bethlehem's true home? Wherever he comes from, we ask that he descend to us, that he come to our forlorn, weary souls. Then may he enjoy his days as the holy child, for soon enough he will become the holy man and learn what true holiness means.

## PRAYER

O holy child of Bethlehem, "be born in us today." If you merely descend to us and show us your holiness by your words, your life, your death, and your rising from the dead, we will marvel, but little will change. Be born not only near us but in us. Make our souls your dwelling place and so transform them that everything about them reflects your rule.

O holy child of Bethlehem, "come to us, abide with us." Remain, stay, take up residence. Nevermore depart from us, for until you rule our souls continually, perpetually, moment to moment and year to year, we will surely forget you as other loves and loyalties call out for our devotion. It has happened before and it will happen again, until you abide with us.

*Amen.*

# 31

# O LOVE, HOW DEEP,
# HOW BROAD, HOW HIGH

Attributed to Thomas à Kempis (ca. 1380-1471)            Suggested tune:
tr. Benjamin Webb (1819-1885)                   *Deus tuorum militum*

O love, how deep, how broad, how high,
beyond all thought and fantasy,
that God, the Son of God, should take
our mortal form for mortals' sake!

For us baptized, for us he bore
his holy fast and hungered sore;
for us temptation sharp he knew,
for us the tempter overthrew.

For us he prayed; for us he taught;
for us his daily works he wrought:
by words and signs and actions thus
still seeking not himself, but us.

For us to evil men betrayed,
scourged, mocked, in purple robe arrayed,
he bore the shameful cross and death;
for us gave up his dying breath.

For us he rose from death again;
for us he went on high to reign;
for us he sent his Spirit here
to guide, to strengthen, and to cheer.

*All glory to our Lord and God*
*for love so deep, so high, so broad—*
*the Trinity, whom we adore*
*for ever and for evermore.*

This is a condensed version of a Latin hymn originally more than twice as long. If not by Thomas à Kempis himself, it originates from the circle surrounding him that practiced what was called the *devotio moderna* (modern devotion), an effort to live humbly, obediently, and simply in fifteenth-century Netherlands. *Deus tuorum militum* was published anonymously in France in 1753.

*O love, how deep, how broad, how high,*
*beyond all thought and fantasy,*
*that God, the Son of God, should take*
*our mortal form for mortals' sake!*

This hymn tells the story of the life of Christ in five stanzas, ending with a Trinitarian doxology. The words "for us" occur twelve times in those six stanzas, indicating the distinguishing characteristic of Christ's life, that all he did was done "for us."

The love expressed in Jesus Christ, says the hymn, is so deep, so broad, so high as to be inconceivable, "beyond all thought and fantasy." It starts with God. Jesus was not merely a good man, a good teacher, the great example. Remarkable as that would have been, it would have originated here, from human

initiative. The life of Jesus began away from here, in the
heart of God. That's why the Nicene Creed says he "came
down from heaven." The Creator and Ruler of the universe
laid power and majesty aside to take "our mortal form for
mortals' sake." It was an act of love—deep, broad, high—from
which everything else in the story of Jesus flows.

*For us baptized, for us he bore*
*his holy fast and hungered sore;*
*for us temptation sharp he knew,*
*for us the tempter overthrew.*

Immediately following Jesus' baptism, an act confirming his
identification with us, Jesus was led into the desert where he
came face to face with the father of lies, another moment of
bonding with us. Jesus meets Satan who offers him power,
fame, and material comforts if Jesus will worship him. The
hymn says these temptations were "sharp" because Christ
wasn't merely God walking around on earth wearing human
flesh as one would wear an overcoat. God had become fully
human, which meant he desired what we desire, fought the
battles we fight, and weighed the compromises and self-
justifications we weigh. But Christ looked Satan in the eye
and said, "Get behind me."

How was Christ's victory over temptation an expression of love
for us? It's not that he provided us an example to emulate, as if
to say, "You can resist temptation, too. Just try a little harder!"
His victory over temptation is our victory because Christ says,
"Come to me. Let us become one, I in you and you in me.
Where I am, you shall be; and as I am, you shall be."

*For us he prayed; for us he taught;*
*for us his daily works he wrought:*

*by words and signs and actions thus*
*still seeking not himself, but us.*

Christians aspire to emulate Christ in living for others, but it's tricky because we easily delude ourselves into thinking we live for others when we're actually living for something else. I once knew a priest who worked himself into an early grave telling himself he lived for others when he was actually acting out his illusion of indispensability. I knew a mother who said she was giving her all for her son when she was actually holding him back for herself. I knew a wife who thought she lived for her husband when she was actually enabling his destructive behavior.

To live for others, we must also take care of ourselves, as Jesus took care of himself. While he never declined to heal the sick or speak a word to strengthen the faint-hearted, he also regularly withdrew for time alone and he declined to go to Jerusalem before he was fully prepared. If Jesus had rushed in to fix every problem and meet every need, he would have been perpetually exhausted, spiritually and emotionally numb, with nothing to give. Only those with a spiritually healthy self have a self to give.

*For us to evil men betrayed,*
*scourged, mocked, in purple robe arrayed,*
*he bore the shameful cross and death;*
*for us gave up his dying breath.*

"No one has greater love than this, to lay down one's life for one's friends," Jesus told the disciples (John 15:13). He then told them they were his friends—he would soon show it by giving his life for them—and commanded them to love one another as he loved them.

Ignatius Loyola, founder of the Jesuit order, embraced
such love when he prayed, "I wish and desire, and it is my
deliberate decision, provided only that it is for your greater
service and praise, to imitate you in bearing all injuries and
affronts, and any poverty, actual as well as spiritual, if your
most holy Majesty desires to choose and receive me into such
a life and state."

*For us he rose from death again;*
*for us he went on high to reign;*
*for us he sent his Spirit here*
*to guide, to strengthen, and to cheer.*

Surprise ending! Christ is risen! Love triumphs after all!
Christ's resurrection was not merely a spectacular miracle
following an exemplary life but the decisive event in a story
that had been building for centuries, perhaps for eons. Good
triumphs over evil!

The story has two epilogues, both referred to in this stanza.
Forty days after Easter, Jesus "went on high to reign." Using
the ancient imagery of the three-storied universe, the
ascension denotes Christ's victory over all things evil, here
and everywhere, now and at all times. What was acted out on
this stage has universal consequences.

The second epilogue has to do with Christ's continuing
presence among us by sending the Holy Spirit to us "to guide,
to strengthen, and to cheer." Christ has sent the Spirit to guide
our steps, to encourage us to act faithfully, and to comfort us
in dark times. We can trust Christ's promise: "I am with you
always, to the very end of the age" (Matthew 28:20).

*All glory to our Lord and God*
*for love so deep, so high, so broad—*
*the Trinity, whom we adore*
*for ever and for evermore.*

It is easy to slip into language that suggests that God has parts (as I have occasionally allowed myself to do in the more fanciful of these meditations). That's what the doctrine of the Trinity has suggested to some people, but they misconstrue it. The Trinity is an attempt to use human language to hint at what is beyond human understanding and expression, namely, that the one, indivisible God is love. Love is an energetic, dynamic, flowing, pulsing thing. It involves giving and receiving. Hence, we speak of "persons" within the one, indivisible God. Such language is inherently and totally inadequate. Boundless, endless, infinite love is too deep, too broad, too high for us to grasp or explain. The doctrine of the Trinity but dimly hints at it.

## PRAYER

When I ponder your life, Lord Jesus, I want to follow in your footsteps, living my life for others as you lived yours for me. But I feel poorly informed and inadequate—and in truth, I often feel unwilling as well. Therefore come and walk beside me, Lord Jesus, and fill me with your Holy Spirit. Tell me again what I need to hear; remind me who you are and what you did for me. Guide me, strengthen me, cheer me, and woo me, Lord. And if necessary, overwhelm me, that I may be wholly yours.

*Amen.*

# 32

# O LOVE THAT WILT NOT LET ME GO

George Matheson (1842-1906)                Suggested tune: *St. Margaret*

*O love that wilt not let me go, I rest my weary soul in thee:*
*I give thee back the life I owe, that in thine ocean depths its flow*
*may richer, fuller be.*

*O light that followest all my way, I yield my flickering torch to thee;*
*my heart restores its borrowed ray, that in thy sunshine's blaze its day*
*may brighter, fairer be.*

*O joy that seekest me through pain, I cannot close my heart to thee;*
*I trace the rainbow through the rain, and feel the promise is not vain,*
*that morn shall tearless be.*

*O cross that liftest up my head, I dare not ask to fly from thee;*
*I lay in dust life's glory dead, and from the ground there*
              *blossoms red*
*life that shall endless be.*

After going blind at the age of eighteen, George Matheson
became a brilliant student at the University of Glasgow
and later a renowned Presbyterian preacher and author of
theological and devotional works. It has been said that he lost

the woman he loved when she broke off their engagement for fear of being married to a blind man. Then, in 1882, when Matheson was forty, his sister married. He later wrote that on his sister's wedding night, he sat alone in his manse and that "something happened" to cause him "the most severe mental suffering." The result was this hymn, written in its entirety in five minutes, Matheson said. *St. Margaret* was composed for this text by Albert Lister Peace, a Scottish musical editor.

*O love that wilt not let me go, I rest my weary soul in thee:*
*I give thee back the life I owe, that in thine ocean depths its flow*
*may richer, fuller be.*

I'm no stranger to weariness. Weariness comes from hard work. And as few physical experiences are more pleasurable than to stretch out on a good mattress when our muscles ache from a day of strenuous labor, few spiritual experiences are more pleasurable than to lie quietly in the arms of God after having exhausted our souls with God's work.

Or at least I thought it was God's work when I was doing it. I told myself it was God's work and others seemed to regard it so. But now I'm not so sure. The only things I'm sure of now are that I exhausted myself doing it and that God now invites me to rest my weary soul in him. Does God invite everyone to do that, even those who never gave a thought to doing his work, who are weary because of a life heedlessly misspent? I hope so.

In the end, I hope we all give back to God the life we owe and discover in his ocean depths a richer, fuller flow than we dreamt possible. May differences fade away as we all find our place in the arms of love that will not let us go. The only difference will then be between those who gladly take their place in those arms and those dragged there against their will. But in the end, I hope even that difference fades away as every wearied soul finds its way home.

*O light that followest all my way, I yield my flickering torch to thee; my heart restores its borrowed ray, that in thy sunshine's blaze its day may brighter, fairer be.*

Though blind from the age of eighteen, George Matheson still envisioned the light that surrounded him when, twenty-two years later, he wrote these words. He may have been thinking back on his youth, when he envisioned his torch as a luminous blaze, only to learn later that the "brighter, fairer" light comes from another source.

I too once envisioned my torch as a luminous blaze. My knowledge of theology, keen intelligence, unflagging dedication, and strong willpower would shine brightly for all to see and appreciate. I was stunned when not everyone fell in line behind me. I now see that what drove me was not faithfulness, but ego—and people probably sensed that. When things began to unravel around me, I thought all was lost. If God had ever been real to me, I now wasn't so sure. Forced to acknowledge that my torch was a flickering wick rather than a luminous blaze, I cried out to a God whose goodness and power I had preached for years but had never really trusted;

I appealed to promises I remembered from long ago but no longer much believed.

Then I discovered the "light that followest all my way," even when my way takes me far afield. God had been with me all along, waiting—waiting for me to stumble, turn around, and look up. I suppose God could have stopped me before I stumbled, but instead God waited. Apparently, I needed to stumble. When I did, my eyes were opened, and I discovered the sunshine of God's face. God had always been with me, for me, waiting. But I had to stop walking by the light of my own faint torch before I could perceive him.

I just now wrote that God waited for me. But in Francis Thompson's poem "The Hound of Heaven," waiting is precisely what God does not do. The poet travels the universe trying to elude God but always hears behind him the relentless pursuing steps of the Hound of Heaven. Finally, exhausted from fleeing, he concludes that all his efforts avail nothing. He admits that "my mangled youth lies dead beneath the heap. My days have crackled and gone up in smoke." Then at last he rests, defeated but content, in the arms of his divine pursuer who says, "All which I took from thee I did but take, not for thy harms, but just that thou might'st seek it in my arms."

So does God wait for us or chase us? Probably both.

> *O joy that seekest me through pain, I cannot close my heart to thee;*
> *I trace the rainbow through the rain, and feel the promise is not vain,*
> *that morn shall tearless be.*

Joy is always seeking us, but it seems that joy is always accompanied by pain. That was certainly George Matheson's experience. Only the spiritually sick seek pain for its own sake, but it is also spiritual sickness to try to avoid all pain. We do that by losing ourselves in work, pleasure, possessions, sports, sex, drugs and alcohol, another person, striving to hold on to our youth, even religious devotion—but joy eludes us. Only in abandonment of self and surrender to the Hound of Heaven is joy found. In Francis Thompson's case as in mine, it was only when the futility of my efforts at self-sufficiency became painful enough that I turned to God. That turning did not eliminate pain, but it subsumed it, and I was able to "trace the rainbow through the rain."

> O cross that liftest up my head, I dare not ask to fly from thee;
> I lay in dust life's glory dead, and from the ground there
>    blossoms red
> life that shall endless be.

The cross of Jesus lifts my weary head. When Jesus saw that I had fallen into the ravine and lay bleeding and helpless, "in dust life's glory dead," he came to me at the great cost of the cross, bandaged my wounds, and lifted my head. Then he carried me to safety, nursed my wounds, and sang the songs of heaven to me. And now from the ground will blossom "red life that shall endless be"—red because of the blood he shed and endless because it is his life.

Jesus has shown that we must go to the back in order to be invited to the front, give in order to receive, die in order to live. That's how it was with him, and that's how it is with us.

## PRAYER

I don't know why you love me, Lord Jesus, or why it was necessary for you to suffer the cross for me, but I shall try to listen, follow, and make every thought, word, and deed an expression of thanks. Enable me to do it faithfully. Lead me to surrender more and more to you, that my heart's "day may brighter, fairer be"—every day brighter, every day fairer, until I am wholly yours.

*Amen.*

# 33

# ONCE TO EVERY MAN AND NATION

James Russell Lowell (1819-1891)                    Suggested tune: *Ebenezer*

Once to every man and nation comes the moment to decide,
in the strife of truth with falsehood, for the good or evil side;
some great cause, some new decision, offering each the bloom
    or blight,
and the choice goes by forever, 'twixt that darkness and that light.

Then to side with truth is noble, when we share her wretched crust,
ere her cause bring fame and profit, and 'tis prosperous to be just;
then it is the brave man chooses while the coward stands aside,
till the multitude make virtue of the faith they had denied.

By the light of burning martyrs, Christ, thy bleeding feet we track,
toiling up new Calv'ries ever with the cross that turns not back;
new occasions teach new duties, time makes ancient good uncouth,
they must upward still and onward, who would keep abreast
    of truth.

Though the cause of evil prosper, yet the truth alone is strong,
though her portion be the scaffold, and upon the throne be wrong,
yet that scaffold sways the future, and behind the dim unknown,
standeth God within the shadow, keeping watch above his own.

These sixteen lines are taken from a poem of ninety lines written by James Russell Lowell in 1845. Lowell was protesting the U.S. Mexican War, which he saw as an act of American aggression to extend the reach of slavery. The tune *Ebenezer* was sung throughout Wales for years before being published for the first time in 1890.

*Once to every man and nation comes the moment to decide,*
*in the strife of truth with falsehood, for the good or evil side;*
*some great cause, some new decision, offering each the bloom*
*    or blight,*
*and the choice goes by forever, 'twixt that darkness and that light.*

Does the moment to decide come but once? Sometimes it does. From some decisions, there's no turning back. After some bad choices, we hurtle downward, unable to right ourselves again, trapped in cages of our own devising.

This hymn says that both individuals and nations make these irreversible decisions, sacrificing their souls for bogus promises. Individuals allow relationships with God and others to wither as they pursue power, prestige, pleasure, and wealth. When those goals either prove elusive or, when attained, fail to deliver the satisfaction promised, these people feel cheated, empty, depressed. Nations—and this hymn was written as a political protest—do the same when fear, xenophobia, and greed define their national life. The destruction and deprivation thus unleashed are often unacknowledged by those who cause them. Putting back together a nation broken by such policies is a daunting and uncertain task.

But sometimes that's not the end of the story. Not every choice goes by forever. Repentance, forgiveness, amendment of life, and a fresh start are often possible.

Years ago I accepted a prestigious position with a large pay package and benefits to match. My life was enjoyable in some respects, but in time, I became angry, isolated, and despondent, cut off from the people and values I held dear. Many a night I lay awake in bed or sat at my desk writing woeful, self-pitying entries in my journal. I felt trapped. But I was not trapped. Eventually I resigned and took another position at half the pay. That decision fed and brought joy to my soul. It was a liberating decision, a born-again experience. I had made a bad choice, but the choice had not gone by forever. Every recovering addict can testify that some poor decisions can be reversed. A life once headed down a destructive path can be salvaged through repentance, surrender to God, and amendment of life.

> Then to side with truth is noble, when we share her wretched crust, ere her cause bring fame and profit, and 'tis prosperous to be just; then it is the brave man chooses while the coward stands aside, till the multitude make virtue of the faith they had denied.

Jesus tasted truth's "wretched crust." He traveled among society's rejects and stooped to succor them. He was rarely welcomed into comfortable homes and had no place to lay his head. Deemed a blasphemer and a threat to law and order, he was executed for treason.

But must it be that way, or can we serve the cause of truth while enjoying more savory fare? Can't the cause of truth occasionally bring fame and profit? I'd like to think there are times when "'tis prosperous to be just."

I tell myself that I've spent my life in the service of truth. I've read the Bible, taught the Bible, preached the Bible. I've been a respected figure in the communities where I've lived. And like Jesus, I have visited the hovels of the destitute—but not often, and I didn't remain there long. More often I have sat on padded cushions while dining at elegant tables and enjoying genteel discussions of poverty and injustice as problems to be addressed by philanthropy and social reform. True, my wife and I support charitable causes and volunteer at a thrift store where we provide goods and services to the poor, but then we return to our comfortable home and our fulsome table. My service to truth has left me unscarred; I have never tracked Jesus' bleeding feet. If I have taken up my cross to follow him, it has been a far lighter cross than his. Have I been "the brave man" or "the coward [who] stands aside?"

> By the light of burning martyrs, Christ, thy bleeding feet we track,
> toiling up new Calv'ries ever with the cross that turns not back;
> new occasions teach new duties, time makes ancient good uncouth,
> they must upward still and onward, who would keep abreast
>     of truth.

It's true that "new occasions teach new duties, time makes ancient good uncouth," but I've never been on the cutting edge of any of that. While others plowed new ground and paved the way for deeper understandings, I usually stood back, cushioned by my safe embrace of conventional views. More often than not, I have come around and accepted the truth uncovered by others' courageous work but only after any threat to me and my reputation was long past. At the heavenly banquet, I won't expect a seat at the head table.

*Though the cause of evil prosper, yet the truth alone is strong, though her portion be the scaffold, and upon the throne be wrong, yet that scaffold sways the future, and behind the dim unknown, standeth God within the shadow, keeping watch above his own.*

Most of what I know, I have learned through trial and error, by stumbling blindly around. Why does the truth so often seem unclear, the "dim unknown"? Must we always wrestle with our souls to discern right and wrong? Why does evil seem so ascendant in the world today? God always seems to stand "within the shadow." If God is truly in charge, why doesn't he fix the world or at least tidy things up a bit?

Dorothy Sayers, the English novelist, considered those questions. Asked why God did not strike a certain dictator dead, she replied, "Why, madam, did he not strike you dumb and imbecile before you uttered that baseless and unkind slander the day before yesterday? Or me, before I behaved with such cruel lack of consideration to that well-meaning friend? And why, sir, did he not cause your hand to rot off at the wrist before you signed your name to that dirty little bit of financial trickery?"

So maybe it's just as well that God stands behind the dim unknown, within the shadow. Maybe he wants us to wrestle with the truth. Moreover, if God spoke unequivocally or intervened to correct every wrong, we wouldn't like it. We like running our lives as we will—and apparently God likes granting us that freedom. Perhaps God wants our love and knows that love cannot be compelled. So God chooses to woo rather than to compel, standing nearby, "within the shadow, keeping watch above his own." God must love ambiguity, for he has created so much of it.

## PRAYER

Fill my mind, O God, with your truth, whether old truth or new. And make my country not only prosperous but holy. Make America good again. Give us all enough clarity and charity to make the next decision a faithful one, and then give us the courage to carry it out and the wisdom to know when and how.

*Amen.*

# 34

## ONWARD, CHRISTIAN SOLDIERS

Sabine Baring-Gould (1834-1924)                    Suggested tune: *St. Gertrude*

Onward, Christian soldiers, marching as to war,
with the cross of Jesus going on before!
Christ the royal Master, leads against the foe;
forward into battle, see his banners go.
Onward, Christian soldiers, marching as to war,
with the cross of Jesus going on before!

At the sign of triumph Satan's host doth flee;
on, then, Christian soldiers, on to victory!
Hell's foundations quiver at the shout of praise;
Christians, lift your voices, loud your anthems raise.
Onward, Christian soldiers, marching as to war,
with the cross of Jesus going on before!

Like a mighty army moves the church of God;
Christians, we are treading where the saints have trod;
we are not divided, all one body we,
one in hope and doctrine, one in charity.
Onward, Christian soldiers, marching as to war,
with the cross of Jesus going on before!

Crowns and thrones may perish, kingdoms rise and wane,
but the church of Jesus constant will remain.
Gates of hell can never 'gainst that church prevail;
we have Christ's own promise, and that cannot fail.

*Onward, Christian soldiers, marching as to war,*
*with the cross of Jesus going on before!*

*Onward, then, ye people, join our happy throng;*
*blend with ours your voices in the triumph song:*
*Glory, laud, and honor, unto Christ the King;*
*this through countless ages we with angels sing:*
*Onward, Christian soldiers, marching as to war,*
*with the cross of Jesus going on before!*

Sabine Baring-Gould, an English priest, educator, and author, wrote this popular hymn in 1865 for children to sing as they walked along a country road. *St. Gertrude* was written six years later by Arthur Sullivan, an English church organist best known for collaborating with librettist W. S. Gilbert to produce a series of popular comic operettas.

*Onward, Christian soldiers, marching as to war,*
*with the cross of Jesus going on before!*
*Christ the royal Master, leads against the foe;*
*forward into battle, see his banners go.*
*Onward, Christian soldiers, marching as to war,*
*with the cross of Jesus going on before!*

Why would we want anyone to march off to war? And if Jesus is the Prince of Peace, why decorate our weapons, shields, and banners with his cross?

War is, very rarely, the lesser evil. Most of those who have started wars thought theirs was one of those rare ones, but history usually disagrees. Few causes for which human blood is spilled seem worth dying for centuries later, and those billed as holy wars are perhaps the most heinous of all, such as the Crusades, carried out with immense sacrifice and suffering in the name of Christ. The slaughter between Roman Catholics and Protestants in the sixteenth century seems horrid in our ecumenically chummy age.

The key word in this hymn is *as*—marching *as* to war. A war, particularly if fought in our homeland, commands our attention. Every decision is made with the war in view. Determining whom to trust becomes a life-or-death matter. War can energize and inspire some people to reach for higher goals and make greater commitments. This hymn asks such energy for the church. What would we do differently if we recognized our decisions as the life-or-death matters they often are? Would we make the same choices if we thought a bullet or grenade might end our lives at any moment? How would things be different if our every word and act reflected our confidence in our Lord's victory and his reign within our hearts?

> *At the sign of triumph Satan's host doth flee;*
> *on, then, Christian soldiers, on to victory!*
> *Hell's foundations quiver at the shout of praise;*
> *Christians, lift your voices, loud your anthems raise.*
> *Onward, Christian soldiers, marching as to war,*
> *with the cross of Jesus going on before!*

"Satan's host" consists not of junior devils, goblins, and fallen angels (though there may be such things), but of pride, self-will, and indifference. And "hell's foundations" are not made of concrete and steel but of attitudes, habits, and priorities. If we focus solely on evils outside ourselves, we run the risk of becoming self-righteous. It is a short step from that to demonizing other people and regarding them as disposable. Nazi Germany is not the only instance of an entire people aligning itself with Satan's host. The past century has seen several other holocausts that differ from the Nazi holocaust only in scale.

While we must combat evil in the wider world, it is the evil growing within us that can destroy us. Often such evil is virtue twisted and distorted or practiced for the wrong reason: We give in order to be admired; our noble work becomes compulsive busyness leading to the neglect of other things; resting becomes laziness; we give well-meaning advice and then demand we be obeyed.

The cure for these things, what will cause Satan's host to flee and hell's foundations to quiver, is to live consciously and intentionally among those whose holy anthems silence competing voices.

> Like a mighty army moves the church of God;
> Christians, we are treading where the saints have trod;
> we are not divided, all one body we,
> one in hope and doctrine, one in charity.
> Onward, Christian soldiers, marching as to war,
> with the cross of Jesus going on before!

The church like a mighty army? More like a mighty turtle, a friend of mine once said. Sometimes it feels as if the church can't move at all. I cannot count the church meetings I have attended that bogged down in disputes about beliefs, procedures, finances, or who's in charge. "We are not divided"? That's not the church I know. In my church, there's plenty of division. Why, I sometimes ask myself, do I continue to put up with it? Why didn't I quit long ago and make my living some other way? I know why: It's the people. Every frustrating one of them is a child of God muddling along, and so am I. Despite our failings and divisions, we're fellow travelers, and we need each other.

Picture Geoffrey Chaucer's motley assortment of pilgrims in *The Canterbury Tales*. They were neither uniform nor single-minded, but neither did they frighten or bore. Each pilgrim was unique. Some lagged behind while others forged ahead. Some traveled as an act of devotion, others for a good time, to make money, because of friends, or for reasons unclear. Some showed nobility of character, some were rascals, most were something in between. Yet all were headed for Canterbury, and most would eventually arrive there.

Armies aren't supposed to muddle along, though. They're supposed to move quickly and purposefully, soldiers in parade, stepping in time, lined up straight, dressed alike. Soldiers are to follow orders without questioning and to express an opinion only when it's asked for. Uniformity, discipline, and obedience are essential lest the army collapse and the cause be lost. But the life of a soldier has its frustrations as well: Some soldiers feel stifled by the limited opportunities for creativity and individual initiative.

It's good to have a few Christian soldiers to fight for the truth lest the rest of us lose sight of it, a few "true believers" to keep us focused on the pilgrim's way and out of the ditches beside the road. But a few Christian soldiers will be enough.

I once sought to be on "the cutting edge" where I would fight the good fight on the front lines, but now I've found a place back on the broad, flat part of the blade where most of the pilgrims are. To be on the cutting edge is also to be on the fringe, isolated from most of the body. I see too much good in too many sorts of people to dissociate myself from them. I may arrive at the kingdom's door later this way, but I'm enjoying the trip and learning a lot from the sundry souls I meet along the way.

Given a choice, I'll take a mighty turtle over a mighty army every time.

> Crowns and thrones may perish, kingdoms rise and wane,
> but the church of Jesus constant will remain.
> Gates of hell can never 'gainst that church prevail;
> we have Christ's own promise, and that cannot fail.
> Onward, Christian soldiers, marching as to war,
> with the cross of Jesus going on before!

Crowns and thrones not only may perish but will perish. They always do. The list of once mighty kingdoms and empires that no longer appear on the map grows longer with each century. But mighty nations usually behave as if their place at the top of the pyramid is justified and permanent, even foreordained. Americans would do well to ponder this. Our day as the world's dominant power may not end soon, but it will end—and possibly soon. Mighty nations and empires not overthrown by competing powers eventually overextend themselves and collapse from atrophy and exhaustion.

The Christian church has sometimes acted like an empire, dressing its leaders in gilded finery, requiring tithes and fees be paid to it, erecting huge buildings that resemble castles, and exiling or killing dissenters. That church is in decline today. Perhaps it is perishing. Perhaps it should.

The church that will not perish is the church of the saints, the holy women and men of every age, most of them long forgotten by the powers of this world. They come from all continents and traditions, differing in every way but one: their humble and faithful service to their Lord. "Gates of hell can never 'gainst that church prevail."

*Onward, then, ye people, join our happy throng;*
*blend with ours your voices in the triumph song:*
*Glory, laud, and honor, unto Christ the King;*
*this through countless ages we with angels sing:*
*Onward, Christian soldiers, marching as to war,*
*with the cross of Jesus going on before!*

On we go, then, marching as to war, singing the triumph song, with the cross of Jesus going on before. We are not a distinguished lot. Ours is a ragtag army; we don't march in step. Some of us aren't sure where we are or where we're going. We are easily distracted. Some have made a wrong turn and are headed in the wrong direction. Most of us can't hear—or don't heed—the voice of our captain.

But we know who our captain is, and we know that at the end of the day, the victory will be his. He doesn't require the best soldiers, only willing soldiers, because the victory depends not on the soldiers but on the captain.

So if soldiers aren't needed, why are there soldiers at all? Why does Christ choose to fight his battles through feckless incompetents when he could summon a squadron of archangels and be done with Satan's host in a nanosecond? The answer is simple yet profound: Christ does not wish to reign alone. He would rather be in our company than sit on his throne attended only by his heavenly host. We are dear to our captain's heart. With us at his side, the victory may be more difficult to attain, but without us at his side, it would be, in our captain's view, no victory at all.

## PRAYER

Lord, teach me when to be still and when to fight; and when I am to fight, may I fight boldly, fairly, and with a forgiving heart.

*Amen.*

# 35

## PRAISE, MY SOUL, THE KING OF HEAVEN

Henry Francis Lyte (1793-1847)                    Suggested tune: *Lauda anima*

Praise, my soul, the King of heaven; to his feet thy tribute bring;
ransomed, healed, restored, forgiven, evermore his praises sing;
Alleluia! Alleluia! Praise the everlasting King.

Praise him for his grace and favor to our forebears in distress;
praise him still the same as ever, slow to chide, and swift to bless:
Alleluia! Alleluia! Glorious in his faithfulness.

Fatherlike he tends and spares us; well our feeble frame he knows;
in his hand he gently bears us, rescues us from all our foes.
Alleluia! Alleluia! Widely yet his mercy flows.

Frail as summer's flower we flourish, blows the wind and it is gone;
but while mortals rise and perish, God endures unchanging on.
Alleluia! Alleluia! Praise the high eternal One.

Angels, help us to adore him; ye behold him face to face;
sun and moon, bow down before him, dwellers all in time and space.
Alleluia! Alleluia! Praise with us the God of grace.

Like Psalm 103 on which it is based, this hymn initially urges the singer's own soul to praise the King of heaven and concludes by bidding the heavenly host to join in the song. Henry Francis Lyte, who also wrote "Abide with me" (see Hymn #2), was born in Scotland but served for years as a priest in a fishing village on the Devonshire coast. *Lauda anima* was composed for this text by John Goss, an English music professor and church organist, and published in 1869.

—⊶⊷—

*Praise, my soul, the King of heaven; to his feet thy tribute bring;*
*ransomed, healed, restored, forgiven, evermore his praises sing;*
*Alleluia! Alleluia! Praise the everlasting King.*

I have a friend who weeps whenever he sings the opening stanza of this hymn. He is a lovely man, gracious and compassionate, but he has hurt people and has been hurt. Ransoming and healing, restoration and forgiveness, are no mere concepts to him. He sings of what he knows.

My friend endured a kind of captivity, not behind bars, but bound by the chains of addiction, desire, and self-will. He felt powerless to escape. He was sick in both body and soul, a disease brought on by his own poor decisions and misdeeds. He felt shabby, like an old cupboard with chipped and water-stained finish, broken glass, rusted hinges, and drawers that stuck on their runners. When, not through his own efforts, recovery came, he experienced it as a kind of ransom, a healing, a restoration. Christ had paid the price for him to be pardoned and set free. He weeps when he sings of it.

*Praise him for his grace and favor to our forebears in distress;*
*praise him still the same as ever, slow to chide, and swift to bless:*
*Alleluia! Alleluia! Glorious in his faithfulness.*

When I read of God's "grace and favor to our forebears in distress," I think of the archetypical story of divine deliverance, the exodus of the Israelites from Egypt over three millennia ago. Even people unfamiliar with the Bible know the story (though perhaps in a Hollywoodish version only partially true to the biblical text). Some modern scholars question the veracity of the biblical text as well. They claim it couldn't have happened as told in the Bible. To them, I reply with a remark a friend of mine likes to make: "Everything in the Bible is true, and some of it actually happened." Biblical truth is about meaning and purpose, what God is up to. A story can convey that truth whether or not it happened precisely as later recorded. It takes on meaning as it is remembered and repeated from generation to generation.

The exodus story is a lens through which Jews and Christians see and interpret God's work in history. Another such lens is provided by the empty tomb, the story of the resurrected Christ. As God has shown "grace and favor to our forebears in distress" time and again throughout history, so he shows grace and favor to us today. He always has and always will.

*Fatherlike he tends and spares us; well our feeble frame he knows;*
*in his hand he gently bears us, rescues us from all our foes.*
*Alleluia! Alleluia! Widely yet his mercy flows.*

God knows our feeble frame because he once had such a frame of his own. He "tends and spares us...gently bears us, and rescues us from all our foes" because he too has known weakness, fear, and foes. Having walked the dusty roads of Palestine and engaged with both the needy and the powerful, God is on intimate terms with suffering, betrayal, and death.

Christians are not the only people who believe in God. Jews and Muslims also believe in a loving and compassionate God, and their level of devotion and commitment puts many Christians to shame. But there is one marvelous difference between God as worshiped by Christians and God as worshiped by everyone else. Our God bleeds. Only the Christian God can say to a grieving, frightened, or dying human being, *"I have walked this way before you and have hallowed every step of it with my blood. I am with you all the way."* This gives an entirely new meaning to words like deity and divine.

> *Frail as summer's flower we flourish, blows the wind and it is gone;*
> *but while mortals rise and perish, God endures unchanging on.*
> *Alleluia! Alleluia! Praise the high eternal One.*

The Bible often notes that human life is brief and fleeting. The image of human flesh resembling the desert flower, blooming quickly when the spring rains come and then fading just as quickly when the hot sun bears down on it, is from Isaiah 40. The psalmist says, "You sweep us away like a dream; we fade away suddenly like the grass" (90:5). Then there is Ecclesiastes, an entire biblical book about the emptiness of human pretensions. It says we pass "like a shadow."

But "God endures unchanging on." One would expect that God, the Creator and Sustainer of all that is, would have no regard for creatures as trifling as human beings: "What is man that you should be mindful of him? the son of man that you should seek him out?" the psalmist asks (8:5). But God's view of who and what is significant is not bound by anyone's expectations, and in the most surprising divine act of all, God visited this little speck of a planet and became a human person.

So has God done other startling things elsewhere? Well...

> *Angels, help us to adore him; ye behold him face to face;*
> *sun and moon, bow down before him, dwellers all in time and space.*
> *Alleluia! Alleluia! Praise with us the God of grace.*

We may never know what God is doing throughout the universe. I think it likely that intelligent beings abound throughout the cosmos, but that's a guess. But whatever beings may exist elsewhere are creatures of the same God who creates us. God creates everything from the smallest subatomic particle to the largest intergalactic cluster. And who knows what created beings may exist outside our universe of time and space?

Has God assumed the flesh of other creatures on other planets as he has assumed our flesh on this one? Perhaps. This too we cannot know, but it would be in keeping with the nature of God as disclosed in Jesus Christ. God's purposes and methods elsewhere are surely consistent with his purposes and methods among us.

That would mean that created beings throughout the universe (and perhaps beyond it) have received their own revelations and perhaps visitations and, in their myriads of voices and tones, join with us to praise their Maker. Perhaps others praise him more faithfully than we do. I hope so. But for now, let us join with whoever may dwell in time and space and with dwellers beyond time and space, with angels and the heavenly host who behold him face to face, to praise our God for his grace and favor.

 **PRAYER**

For how many things shall I sing your praises, gracious God? That you have ransomed, healed, restored, and forgiven me. That you have done the same for generations before me and will do so for generations after me. That you are "slow to chide and swift to bless." That when we fall, you bear us up. That you invite us to join our voices with the rest of your creation to praise you: "Holy, holy, holy Lord, God of power and might, heaven and earth are full of your glory. Hosanna in the highest."

*Amen.*

# 36

## TAKE MY LIFE AND LET IT BE

Frances Ridley Havergal (1836-1879)                    Suggested tune: *Hendon*

Take my life, and let it be consecrated, Lord, to thee;
take my moments and my days, let them flow in ceaseless praise.
Take my hands, and let them move at the impulse of thy love;
take my feet, and let them be swift and beautiful for thee.

Take my voice, and let me sing always, only, for my King;
take my lips, and let them be filled with messages from thee.
Take my silver and my gold; not a mite would I withhold.
Take my intellect, and use every power as thou shalt choose.

Take my will, and make it thine: it shall be no longer mine.
Take my heart, it is thine own; it shall be thy royal throne.
Take my love, my Lord, I pour at thy feet its treasure store.
Take myself, and I will be ever, only, all for thee.

This hymn is a series of couplets, each expressing an
aspect of the opening couplet, with the final one summing
up the whole. Frances Ridley Havergal was an English
poet, musician, and linguist, the daughter of an Anglican

clergyman. Her life is said to have exemplified the words of this hymn. *Hendon* is by Henri A. César Malan, a Swiss composer. It was published in 1827.

---

*Take my life, and let it be consecrated, Lord, to thee;*
*take my moments and my days, let them flow in ceaseless praise.*
*Take my hands, and let them move at the impulse of thy love;*
*take my feet, and let them be swift and beautiful for thee.*

You have given me, O God, all that I am and have and know. Every relationship, every opportunity, every task, even my ability to make decisions and plan for the future, is a gift from you. You dreamt it all up in your imagination and then called it into being. Then you dreamt of me, called me into being, and placed me in the midst of it. In thanksgiving to you, I now give back to you all that you have given me. Consecrate it, O my God, and use it as you will, for your purposes and your glory.

Thank you that I have once again awakened to greet the sunrise and to contemplate the hours that stretch before me. Thank you for the people I expect to see and speak to, the decisions I expect to make, the places I intend to go, the challenges awaiting me, and the tasks I hope to accomplish. Whatever comes to me this day, let every moment flow in ceaseless praise to you.

These hands have grown old now, wrinkled and spotted. Most of what these hands will have done, they have already done; little remains for them yet to do. Bless, O God, what these hands have done, all the people they have held and touched, the words they have written and typed, the toys they have played with, the gardens they have tended, the transactions they have effected, the tasks they have accomplished or failed to accomplish. Where my hands have done amiss, forgive and redeem. And in what few things these hands may yet address themselves to, "let them move at the impulse of thy love."

To how many places these old feet have carried me! Bless every spot my soles have touched—office, street, car, church, home, hospital, school, bed, farm, mountainside, seashore, and river bottom. And wherever these feet will take me today, make it a holy place, by my presence there, if it may be. Bar my way to places where I might forget that I am accountable to you. May my feet even now carry me where you shall choose and where I best may serve and glorify you.

*Take my voice, and let me sing always, only, for my King;*
*take my lips, and let them be filled with messages from thee.*
*Take my silver and my gold; not a mite would I withhold.*
*Take my intellect, and use every power as thou shalt choose.*

I've experienced the human tongue as "a restless evil, full of deadly poison" (James 3:8), both as the recipient and as the dispenser of the tongue's poison. Words have hurt me. I also remember times when I have hurt another, using my verbal skills to belittle, embarrass, or assert my imagined superiority and claims over those of others. Forgive me, O God, for misusing my verbal gifts. And now, I pray, "take my voice and let me sing always, only, for my King," that every word may be worthy of one claiming the name of Christ. I call to mind the people with whom I expect to talk today—family, business associates, sales clerks and waiters, the homeless on the street, people at the other end of the telephone. And I call to mind those with whom I shall communicate in other ways, by writing, email, body language, and facial expression. May every communication from me be a communication from you, O my God.

Give me also attentive ears that I may hear what others are telling me, especially if I resist hearing it for reasons that are not of you.

I'm not so sure about the silver and gold part. Surely, O God, I can spend money for my own needs and the enjoyment of what you have provided. Do I really want to give everything to you? True, it all comes from you and belongs to you—but I like silver and gold and what they make possible. How about if you take a lot of my silver and gold, but I hold back enough to use or look at now and then?

As for my intellect, I'd love to turn that over to you. But how? My intellect has been rebelling for years. It questions everything, accepts nothing, and tends toward a cynical nihilism. I think (there it is again—I do too much thinking) the way to surrender my intellect is to let it wander where it will but to pay it little heed. Faith is not a matter of the intellect, anyway, but of trusting you, O God, and trusting is a choice I can make no matter the errant thoughts that flit through my mind. I shall ignore them while I get on with trusting you. At least I think I will.

*Take my will, and make it thine: it shall be no longer mine.*
*Take my heart, it is thine own; it shall be thy royal throne.*
*Take my love, my Lord, I pour at thy feet its treasure store.*
*Take myself, and I will be ever, only, all for thee.*

Now I come to the main thing. Call it the will or call it the heart. I have learned to appear faithful to many who know me, O God, but my good behavior doesn't always reflect what is within me. There's no pretending on the inside, where my heart is open to you and all my desires known.

What you get in me, dear God, is a deeply divided will and heart. I am lured both toward you and away from you. I offer my tepid heart and my conflicted will to you with as much honesty and sincerity as I can, and I ask that you increase the honesty and sincerity with which I make this offering. I know I shall resist your advances, but take from me every shred of self-will. I am frightened as I invite you to do this, O God, for I know neither what form your advances will take nor how entrenched my resistance will be. But I ask you now to break my resistance. Move in upon me, capture me, imprison me, and bind me, for only when you hold me in your arms so that I cannot escape will I be truly free.

Take my love, my God, "I pour at thy feet its treasure store." I love so many things. May I see and love you in all my loves, in my wife and family and friends, in my work and leisure, my moments and my days, my thoughts and desires. Be present and be loved in all that I know and think and do. I pour it all at your feet. Deepen and refine my love for the world you have made and for you, as you come to me through the world you have made.

## PRAYER

Take myself, O God, all that I am and ever will be, that I may be ever, only, all for you. Always, totally, all of me, everything. Having now reviewed and examined myself and my life, I lay all at your feet, holding nothing back. Consecrate me, O God, and make me your own.

*Amen.*

# 37

# THE CHURCH'S ONE FOUNDATION

Samuel J. Stone (1839-1900)                    Suggested tune: *Aurelia*

*The church's one foundation is Jesus Christ her Lord;*
*she is his new creation by water and the word.*
*From heaven he came and sought her to be his holy bride;*
*with his own blood he bought her, and for her life he died.*

*Elect from every nation, yet one o'er all the earth,*
*her charter of salvation, one Lord, one faith, one birth,*
*one holy name she blesses, partakes one holy food,*
*and to one hope she presses, with every grace endued.*

*Though with a scornful wonder, men see her sore oppressed,*
*by schisms rent asunder, by heresies distressed,*
*yet saints their watch are keeping; their cry goes up, "How long?"*
*And soon the night of weeping shall be the morn of song.*

*Mid toil and tribulation, and tumult of her war,*
*she waits the consummation of peace forevermore;*
*till, with the vision glorious, her longing eyes are blessed,*
*and the great church victorious shall be the church at rest.*

*Yet she on earth hath union with God the Three in One,*
*and mystic sweet communion with those whose rest is won.*
*O happy ones and holy! Lord, give us grace that we,*
*like them, the meek and lowly, on high may dwell with thee.*

Surprisingly, this great hymn of Christian unity, written in 1865, was intended as a partisan statement in a controversy that once rattled the Church of England. John Colenso, a bishop from South Africa, had written a book questioning the historical accuracy of portions of the Old Testament. Traditionalists saw this as an attack on biblical truth and Samuel J. Stone, a high-church Anglican priest, wrote this hymn to defend the traditionalist position. It is based on the creedal affirmation of the "one holy catholic and apostolic church." After the Colenso controversy blew over, however, one polemical stanza was dropped from the hymn, and the rest was soon embraced by Christians of many hues as an expression of the unity for which all Christians strive. *Aurelia*, published in 1864, was written by Samuel Sebastian Wesley, grandson of Charles Wesley (see Hymns #20, 24, 25, 28).

*The church's one foundation is Jesus Christ her Lord;*
*she is his new creation by water and the word.*
*From heaven he came and sought her to be his holy bride;*
*with his own blood he bought her, and for her life he died.*

I recently attended a church meeting on a controversial topic where everyone passionately espoused the same point of view. I realized that it didn't matter which side we were on. Either way, the tone would have been the same. We were all true believers, single-minded, and satisfied. Totally certain of ourselves, we didn't budge because we saw no need to budge. Only people who disagreed with us needed to budge.

We had lost sight of our foundation, forgetting that "no one can lay any foundation other than the one that has been laid; that foundation is Jesus Christ" (1 Corinthians 3:11). If asked, most of us would have said that we based not only our opinions but also our lives on the foundation of Jesus Christ. Since we were sure we hadn't slipped off that foundation, we never stopped patting ourselves on the back long enough to pray for Christ's guidance, much less to submit our opinions and our lives to his rule. We had in fact signed on with another ruler, namely ourselves. We knew right from wrong, truth from falsehood, and expected Christ to fall in line beneath our banner.

It's just the reverse, of course. The church is Christ's creation and accountable to him, not the other way around. Beginning with the water of baptism, Christ recreates us and solders us to himself: Where he leads, we are to follow. And by the word—read, preached, heard, and received—we grow in grace and daily learn what it means to follow faithfully.

In imagery derived from the Book of Revelation (21:1-4), this hymn envisions Christ leaving his home in heaven to enter the world in search of his beloved, the church. Even with its bumbling failures, the church is the object of Christ's love, and Christ makes an "until we are parted by death" pledge to us. Then, to seal his pledge, he goes the ultimate distance and dies for us, but it turns out to be "until we are united by death," for Christ's death secures our place in his arms.

*Elect from every nation, yet one o'er all the earth,*
*her charter of salvation, one Lord, one faith, one birth,*
*one holy name she blesses, partakes one holy food,*
*and to one hope she presses, with every grace endued.*

I have some experience of the "from every nation" aspect of Christ's church, having spent several months serving a parish in England and several months teaching at a theological school in Nigeria. I studied in Zimbabwe and have worshiped in more than a dozen countries. Christians with whom I would seem to have little in common have warmly embraced me and taught me much. Their wisdom, courage, and faithfulness humble me. Our differences are not eliminated but encompassed by our "one Lord, one faith, one birth."

Every week I partake of that "one holy food." It's hard for me to perceive Christ in the sacrament. But then how would I expect Christ to come to me? Through a bush that burns but is not consumed? A voice in the middle of the night? A blinding light beside the road? I would doubt those signs as well, so why not bread and wine?

The one hope to which we press is that we may rest in Christ's embrace. To that end, we pray that the church, indeed the whole creation, be "with every grace endued" so that even the most recalcitrant and rebellious among us may finally find a place in Christ's arms, infused with his beauty and love.

> Though with a scornful wonder, men see her sore oppressed,
> by schisms rent asunder, by heresies distressed,
> yet saints their watch are keeping; their cry goes up, "How long?"
> And soon the night of weeping shall be the morn of song.

We're a long way from the hope mentioned in the previous stanza. People have good reason to gaze upon the church "with a scornful wonder," and having spent my life within the church, I know those reasons better than someone looking on from outside. Schisms and heresies aren't the only things that oppress us—there's our hypocrisy, our obsession with trivialities, our navel-gazing, our listless witnessing. Schisms and heresies are part of a larger picture that provokes scornful wonder. So much we have to repent of!

Technically, I am not a schismatic. I have remained in communion with my brother and sister Christians when others have broken fellowship and refused to worship alongside us. But that doesn't mean I've been faithful. Faithfulness is not about technical correctness but about an obedient, open, embracing, forgiving heart. When I have thought or spoken disparagingly of others, I have become a schismatic in all but the technical sense.

Then there's heresy. Heresy is false belief, or at best, an overemphasis on some part of the truth to the neglect of other parts. I have always been a heretic. I suspect all Christians have entertained heresy at some point. Our tiny minds understand almost nothing, and what we do understand, we barely understand. Everything I have ever said or written may be shot through with heresy, and if someone wants to look on that with a scornful wonder, then so be it. But God has always used schismatics, heretics, and other sinners to achieve his purposes. That is God's way, and the Christian church is perhaps the foremost example of God's fondness for flawed instruments. That is indeed a wonder—a blessed wonder, not a scornful one.

*Mid toil and tribulation, and tumult of her war,*
*she waits the consummation of peace forevermore;*
*till, with the vision glorious, her longing eyes are blessed,*
*and the great church victorious shall be the church at rest.*

I cannot recall a time when the world didn't seem to be in toil, tribulation, and tumult. The church often feels that way as well. It seems we shall be awaiting "the consummation of peace forevermore" forevermore. That peace will come only after the peoples of the world, all of us, have learned humility and charity. It will require abandoning national and ethnic pride and military and economic imperialism. Convincing us to turn to humility and charity may require violence and pain. It may come only after our greed and pride have caused devastating environmental destruction and wiped out entire cultures. I pray not. I pray that our learning to live peacefully may be peaceful. Lord, teach us what we need to learn to usher in peace forevermore, and, if possible, teach us gently.

*Yet she on earth hath union with God the Three in One,*
*and mystic sweet communion with those whose rest is won.*
*O happy ones and holy! Lord, give us grace that we,*
*like them, the meek and lowly, on high may dwell with thee.*

Christians are to be both happy and holy. The well-known author Madeleine L'Engle said the distinguishing mark of a Christian is joy. That will come as a surprise to those who have known only Christians whose outlook was pinched and negative. I wouldn't say those people aren't real Christians, but they have yet to discover what the faith they espouse means. Mature Christians are invariably joyful. Saint Paul wrote joyfully from a prison cell. Christians are joyful because they are holy. Holiness isn't a matter of being or doing good but of being set apart from a world often characterized by toil, tribulation, and tumult. That setting apart is centered in the heart and will, not in anything seen or measurable on the outside.

Meekness and lowliness also characterize the church. Some think of that as groveling. Not so. We're talking about humility, knowing who you are and who you aren't and knowing who God is and who God isn't. Humble people have a grasp on reality that distinguishes them from the world at large and leads to the joy that is the chief characteristic of a Christian. Only grace, the infusion of God's power into the human soul, makes any of this possible.

 **PRAYER**

Give us grace, O God, that we, like the happy and holy, like the meek and lowly, on high may dwell with thee.

*Amen.*

# 38

## THE DAY THOU GAVEST, LORD, IS ENDED

John Ellerton (1826-1893)                    Suggested tune: *St. Clement*

*The day thou gavest, Lord, is ended,*
*the darkness falls at thy behest;*
*to thee our morning hymns ascended,*
*thy praise shall sanctify our rest.*

*We thank thee that thy church, unsleeping*
*while earth rolls onward into light,*
*through all the world her watch is keeping,*
*and rests not now by day or night.*

*As o'er each continent and island*
*the dawn leads on another day,*
*the voice of prayer is never silent,*
*nor dies the strain of praise away.*

*The sun that bids us rest is waking*
*your people 'neath the western sky,*
*and hour by hour fresh lips are making*
*thy wondrous doings heard on high.*

*So be it, Lord; thy throne shall never,*
*like earth's proud empires, pass away;*
*thy kingdom stands, and grows for ever*
*till all thy creatures own thy sway.*

This hymn is based on Psalm 113:3: "From the rising of the
sun to its going down let the Name of the LORD be praised."
Some have dismissed this hymn for its association with
the piety of Victorian England and the British Empire on
which the sun was said never to set. Queen Victoria chose
it to be sung at her Diamond Jubilee in 1897. Moreover,
it was written as a missionary hymn when the Church of
England was evangelizing the world in the wake of British
imperialism. All that aside, however, the hymn conveys an
admirable sense of what English music scholar Eric Routley
has called the "settled, orderly, decent family worship in
a well-rooted society." Only the first stanza marks it as an
evening hymn. John Ellerton was a British clergyman.
*St. Clement* was composed for this text by Clement C.
Scholefield and published in 1874.

*The day thou gavest, Lord, is ended,*
*the darkness falls at thy behest;*
*to thee our morning hymns ascended,*
*thy praise shall sanctify our rest.*

"Thank you, Father, for the gift of another bonus day" is my
first prayer every morning upon awakening. That's because at
my age, every day I awaken healthy and whole is a bonus not
granted to everyone. As the day fades away, I thank God for
it again. I can no longer affect it in any way. It belongs now

(as in fact it always belonged) to God. I ask that God carry forward the work I did during the day, correcting what went amiss and building upon what went right, and I ask that God deliver me from obsessing about what I cannot change. My mind, my muscles, and my soul are ready for rest.

The darkness falls at God's behest. As God has given the night to me, I now give it back to God and ask that God make it a holy night. The darkness can be a restful time, preparing me for another day, but it is also a time when demons roam and shameful acts are done in secret. Deliver me and those I love, I pray, from the hands of demons and from any desire buried within us to join their ranks. "Sanctify our rest."

*We thank thee that thy church, unsleeping*
*while earth rolls onward into light,*
*through all the world her watch is keeping,*
*and rests not now by day or night.*

I like the image of the unsleeping church keeping watch all day and all night, every day and every night, through all the world, but that's not a church I recognize. My experience is of a church that often dozes off when it should be vigilant, is distracted by unimportant things while neglecting essentials, and stumbles along not knowing where it is, where it's going, or where it should be going. That's pretty much a description of me as well, and when I'm in church I'm surrounded by others of a similar bent. I can't pretend we're ever vigilant, never sleeping.

Yet these words are not a complete fiction because God makes use of this tepid devotion. I believe I am a more grounded disciple than I once was, and it has been largely through the witness of ordinary Christians that I came to this groundedness. Yes, I've crossed paths with a few luminous saints, both in person and in print, and they have influenced me as well, but it's the unheralded faith of my parents and grandparents, my teachers, and my colleagues at the office, on the street, and in the pews around me that has nudged me along and held me up. They may have been as bumbling, confused, and listless as I was, but they are the church I love. And God loves it, too.

> As o'er each continent and island
> the dawn leads on another day,
> the voice of prayer is never silent,
> nor dies the strain of praise away.

These words remind me of the prayer offered seven times a day in Benedictine abbeys the world over, to say nothing of hundreds of thousands of parish churches. And of course Christians aren't the only people praying. Included in that voice of prayer that's never silent are the prayers and praises of all God's children: Jews praying the Shema, Muslims prostrating themselves on their prayer rugs, Buddhists with their prayer wheels, and Hindus addressing the multiple expressions of divinity offered by their faith. And there will always be a desperate soul somewhere, perhaps someone with no faith at all, pleading for relief or deliverance.

God is too great to be fully comprehended by any one person or faith tradition. When we pray, we join our voices with billions of others whose experiences of God differ from ours. I have learned much and been helpfully humbled by my study of the great luminaries of other faiths, and I hope that in

God's time, we will all link arms in that place where sorrow
and pain are no more, neither sighing, but life everlasting.

*The sun that bids us rest is waking*
*our brethren 'neath the western sky,*
*and hour by hour fresh lips are making*
*thy wondrous doings heard on high.*

As the sun moves ever westward beyond the horizon,
every early morning ray shines on people raising their
hands in praise. Hour by hour, day by day, millennium by
millennium, as generation succeeds generation, on every
continent and island, God's people continually sing his
praises. They praise him in their own languages and with
their own music, fresh lips every day adding their praises to
the chorus that has been singing uninterruptedly for as long
as human voices have been heard. Those voices bicker over
other, lesser things, but when they put lesser things aside,
they join in a united choir to praise and glorify the God who
creates all sound. That is the Christian church doing what it
is meant to do.

When I let my imagination roam freely, I envision other
creatures and beings—angels and archangels, suns and moons,
tiny atoms and giant galaxies, intelligent beings of whom we
know nothing—adding their voices to complete that chorus.
Confined as we are to one tiny planet in a remote outpost of
the universe, how can we know the extent of God's praise?

*So be it, Lord; thy throne shall never,*
*like earth's proud empires, pass away;*
*thy kingdom stands, and grows for ever*
*till all thy creatures own thy sway.*

"So be it, Lord." This is perhaps the most profound prayer one can utter. To say "So be it, Lord" is to acknowledge our place in the universe and let God be God.

Every day I pray for the time when "all thy creatures own thy sway," the time when God's will is done on earth as it is in heaven, the Peaceable Kingdom with the leopard lying down with the kid, the calf and the lion and the fatling together, led by a little child (Isaiah 11:6-9). I don't know how or when it shall come to be (the daily newscasts give no hint of its imminent arrival), but it's a matter of faith that it shall be and a matter of faithfulness to work to bring it to pass. And then we must leave it, as we leave all things, in God's hands. So be it, Lord.

## PRAYER

Guide us waking, O Lord, and guard us sleeping; that awake we may watch with Christ, and asleep we may rest in peace.

*Amen.*

# 39

## WHEN I SURVEY THE WONDROUS CROSS

Isaac Watts (1674-1748)                Suggested tunes: *Hamburg, Rockingham*

When I survey the wondrous cross
where the young Prince of glory died,
my richest gain I count but loss,
and pour contempt on all my pride.

Forbid it, Lord, that I should boast,
save in the death of Christ my God!
All the vain things that charm me most,
I sacrifice them to his blood.

See from his head, his hands, his feet,
sorrow and love flow mingled down!
Did e'er such love and sorrow meet,
or thorns compose so rich a crown?

Were the whole realm of nature mine,
That were an offering far too small;
love so amazing, so divine,
demands my soul, my life, my all.

—⚯—

Congregationalist preacher Isaac Watts is known as the Father of English Hymnody. Prior to his day, singing in English churches—when there was singing—was dreary and limited largely to the psalms and other biblical passages. "The singing of God's praise is the part of worship most closely related to heaven, but its performance among us is the worst on earth," Watts said. To remedy this, he wrote both original hymns and metric poems based on the psalms that could be sung to familiar tunes. This hymn is perhaps his most beloved, sung by Christians of all denominations the world over. It is based on Galatians 6:14: "May I never boast of anything except the cross of our Lord Jesus Christ, by which the world has been crucified to me, and I to the world." It was published in 1707. *Hamburg* is by Lowell Mason, published in 1824. *Rockingham* is by Edward Miller, published in 1790.

*When I survey the wondrous cross*
*where the young Prince of glory died,*
*my richest gain I count but loss,*
*and pour contempt on all my pride.*

When I survey the wondrous cross, I see works of art: a pendant or brooch, the ornament atop a steeple or tower, a needlepointed kneeler or appliqued vestment, a painting or carving. But the cross was not at first a work of art. Surveying that first cross was like staring at a noose, an electric chair, or a guillotine.

The young Prince of glory died on that cross, the man above all others who least deserved a tortured death. The church teaches that his death won for me "my richest gain," but how was that so? Why did the Prince of glory have to die like that? Was there no other way? I don't understand and perhaps I never will, but it's not a matter of understanding. So I continue to sing this song, "pour contempt on all my pride," and stand with Saint Paul in counting all things as rubbish that I may gain Christ (Philippians 3:8).

But do I mean what I sing? If "my richest gain I count but loss," why do I spend so much energy on vanities like my physical fitness and appearance, my finances, learning new things, and satisfying my artistic taste? Would I really give up all that, count it all as loss, in order to gain Christ, or does the warmth I feel as I sing this hymn arise from a sentimental, nodding approval of values I have no intention of actually embracing?

*Forbid it, Lord, that I should boast,*
*save in the death of Christ my God!*
*All the vain things that charm me most,*
*I sacrifice them to his blood.*

Boast? I needn't ask God to forbid my boasting, for boasting is unseemly and I never want to appear unseemly. So I don't boast. Rather, I try to appear humble, hoping people will recognize my stellar gifts without my having to point them out. Vain things do charm me. I wouldn't devote so much attention to them if they didn't charm me. But boast? Certainly not.

Would God really forbid me to boast about vain things? God
has given me freedom to boast or not to boast and to forbid
my boasting would cancel that. I'd become a mere robot, a
computer, or a puppet. Surely God doesn't want that, and
neither do I. So I ask that God make the death of Christ my
God so vivid and compelling a reality to me that beside it,
"all the vain things that charm me most" will appear as the
worthless trinkets they are.

> See from his head, his hands, his feet,
> sorrow and love flow mingled down!
> Did e'er such love and sorrow meet,
> or thorns compose so rich a crown?

I see your blood, Lord, flowing down from your head, your
hands, your feet. I want to say something to you, but I can't.
I'm afraid to speak. My tongue grows thick and numb, and
the words stick in my throat. All I can do is stand here and
watch your blood ooze out, run down your arms and legs,
and clot in your hair and beard. Why do I stay here? I'd
rather be somewhere else. This is an eerie, heavy place. Why
can't I bring myself to leave?

Love and sorrow mingled, meeting. That's what I see in your
bloody flesh, Lord, and that's what rivets me here. You said
that no one has any greater love than to lay down his life for
his friends, and now I'm watching you do it. Let those two
things, your love and your sorrow, mingle and meet in me as
they do in you—love that will stop at nothing for the sake of
the beloved and sorrow at what that love required of you.

Is it always like that? Does love always require suffering? I
think so, because genuine love identifies with the beloved;

when the beloved hurts, the lover also hurts. But your suffering, Lord Jesus, is far greater than love usually requires, not only because the circumstances of your dying were so grim, but also because, in some way that I don't understand, you bear as well the suffering that otherwise would be mine. You bleed in place of me, while I watch in place of you.

*Were the whole realm of nature mine,*
*That were an offering far too small;*
*love so amazing, so divine,*
*demands my soul, my life, my all.*

F. A. Iremonger, in his biography of the late archbishop of Canterbury William Temple, tells a moving story about the closing stanza of this hymn.

A sophisticated, intellectual skepticism and religious indifference were in vogue at Oxford University in 1931. The few committed Christians on campus invited Temple, then archbishop of York and already a renowned author, to lead a weeklong preaching mission. Not a seat was to be had in St. Mary's Church. Students, some of them committed Christians but many merely curious, sat on the floor and around the pulpit and stood in the church entryway. Temple eschewed the emotional appeals favored by many evangelists. Night after night, he delivered a thoughtful defense of Christian faith as a coherent and challenging philosophy of life.

Temple issued no altar call. Only once did he ask for a response. At the conclusion of his last address, he asked the congregation to sing this hymn but interrupted the singing before this final stanza. "I want you to read over this verse before you sing it," Temple said. "These are tremendous words. If you don't mean them, keep silent. If you mean them even a little, but want to mean them more, sing them very softly." There was a dead silence as every eye fastened on the hymn text. Then the church was filled with the voices of 2,000 young men and women singing this stanza in a whisper.

The spark for dozens of later Christian vocations was struck that night. One man recalled it as "an experience never to be erased from my memory till the whole tablet is blotted."

 **PRAYER**

Lord Jesus, may I see you so clearly that I lose the desire to gaze on anything else. Be all in all to me, Lord, that when I take pleasure in something of this world, I do it as an act of praise because through it you disclose to me some hint of yourself. And if ever I must choose between you and the things that charm me most, give me the wisdom and courage to let all else go and cling solely to you.

*Amen.*

# 40

## WHERE CROSS THE CROWDED WAYS OF LIFE

Frank Mason North (1850-1935)          Suggested tune : *Gardiner*

*Where cross the crowded ways of life,*
*where sound the cries of race and clan,*
*above the noise of selfish strife,*
*we hear your voice, O Son of Man.*

*In haunts of wretchedness and need,*
*on shadowed thresholds fraught with fears,*
*from paths where hide the lures of greed,*
*we catch the vision of your tears.*

*From tender childhood's helplessness,*
*from human grief and burdened toil,*
*from famished souls, from sorrow's stress,*
*your heart has never known recoil.*

*The cup of water given for you*
*still holds the freshness of your grace;*
*yet long these multitudes to view*
*the sweet compassion of your face.*

*O Master, from the mountainside,*
*make haste to heal these hearts of pain;*
*among these restless throngs abide;*
*O tread the city's streets again...*

*...till all the world shall learn your love,*
*and follow where your feet have trod,*
*till glorious from your heaven above*
*shall come the city of our God.*

Frank Mason North, a Methodist pastor in New York City, worked to address the poverty and alienation occasioned by the Industrial Revolution. He was an early advocate for women's rights, child labor laws, and workers' rights to organize. His hymn vividly describes scenes found even today in major urban centers the world over. It is an early—and one of the most poignant—expressions of the social gospel. *Gardiner* was composed by William Gardiner, a nineteenth-century British hosiery manufacturer.

*Where cross the crowded ways of life,*
*where sound the cries of race and clan,*
*above the noise of selfish strife,*
*we hear your voice, O Son of Man.*

I like silence. It relaxes me and helps me focus my thoughts. I like places with no television and no idle chatter. My cellphone and my car radio are often turned off. It's in those quiet moments that I find it easiest to hear the voice of Jesus. But I know silence is a luxury that I am privileged to choose. Many people do not have that option. For them, "the cries of race and clan" and "the noise of selfish strife" fill every moment. Can they hear Jesus' voice too? Yes. It's harder to hear Jesus amidst the world's clamor and clatter, but he is there. Perhaps he spends more time there than in those quiet places where I seek him.

*In haunts of wretchedness and need,*
*on shadowed thresholds fraught with fears,*
*from paths where hide the lures of greed,*
*we catch the vision of your tears.*

Is it "the lures of greed" that create the world's "haunts of wretchedness and need" and its "shadowed thresholds fraught with tears?" Yes, but not entirely—poor decisions by the victims often play a part as well. But those of us with two cars in our garages, two televisions in our homes, and closets full of clothing we rarely wear, who live comfortably insulated from the haunts of wretchedness and need and the shadowed thresholds fraught with tears and yet feel no responsibility to address them, might want to take a long look in the mirror when we say our prayers. Perhaps we will glimpse the face of Jesus standing behind us and catch a vision of his tears.

*From tender childhood's helplessness,*
*from human grief and burdened toil,*
*from famished souls, from sorrow's stress,*
*your heart has never known recoil.*

In her early years as a sophisticated skeptic who pooh-poohed organized religion, Dorothy Day, founder of the Catholic Worker movement, could not fathom why poor and powerless refugees arriving in New York from a Europe devastated by World War I flocked to the church for solace when the church hierarchy seemed so impervious to their needs.

But their longing for the church had nothing to do with its hierarchy. The destitute flocked to the church because of

Jesus, who said, "Come to me, all you that are weary and are carrying heavy burdens, and I will give you rest" (Matthew 11:28). Overlooked and perhaps even blamed for their condition by those passing by them, those refugees were never overlooked by Jesus. He knew them each by name, and he knew where to find them. And they knew he knew.

> The cup of water given for you
> still holds the freshness of your grace;
> yet long these multitudes to view
> the sweet compassion of your face.

No doubt Jesus' healing the sick and feeding the hungry drew people to him. But I suspect the main thing Jesus offered was himself, the "sweet compassion" of his face. The destitute not only suffer from physical want, but they also feel unneeded, worthless, like refuse. By giving of himself, Jesus endowed them with a dignity and worth most had never known before.

I once knew a bishop who had many failings as an administrator but was beloved by everyone who knew him. Many told how he gave them his undivided attention for as long as they were with him. Even those forced to sit outside his office until 4 p.m. for a 2 p.m. appointment (because the person with the previous appointment held the bishop's attention so completely that he never glanced at his watch) sang his praises because when they finally saw him, they felt an acceptance and spiritual embrace like no other. That bishop didn't just do things for people; he gave himself to people.

I don't discount the importance of good administration, but I'm grateful that when God came to us in person, it wasn't to teach us administrative skills.

*O Master, from the mountainside,*
*make haste to heal these hearts of pain;*
*among these restless throngs abide;*
*O tread the city's streets again...*

Jesus had just heard the voice on the Mount of the
Transfiguration say to three of his disciples, "This is my
Son, the Beloved; listen to him!" (Mark 9:7). The disciples
wanted to remain on the mountaintop, even offering to
construct residences there. But Jesus led them down from the
mountain to find their work and calling in the valley below.
Jesus declined to remain in a place where he must have felt
hugely affirmed and comfortable, choosing instead to return
with his disciples to the "hearts of pain" and the "restless
throngs." It was among them that he was most at home.

*...till all the world shall learn your love,*
*and follow where your feet have trod,*
*till glorious from your heaven above*
*shall come the city of our God.*

Years ago I served at a downtown parish in Charleston, West
Virginia. Our location brought many indigent and homeless
people to our door. I soon became jaded and stopped
believing their tales of misfortune, but I gave them what
they asked for, usually something to eat, a night's lodging,
gasoline, or a bus ticket out of town. I confess that one
reason I gave it to them was to get rid of them.

One morning a bedraggled man appeared and told a
particularly implausible story. He said he was a producer of
television commercials and had produced one to sell used
cars. He had already tried in vain to sell his commercial to

dealerships in Chicago, Indianapolis, Louisville, Lexington, Huntington, and Charleston. Would I advance him the money for a bus ticket to Roanoke, the next television market? He promised to send the money back when he sold his commercial. The man's geography made sense, but I'd heard such promises before and after buying dozens of bus tickets had received not so much as a thank-you note in return. But I bought him the ticket. Ten days later, I was astonished to receive a postal money order for twice the cost of the ticket, with a note from that man telling me he had sold his commercial to an auto dealer in Roanoke and wanted not only to repay his debt but also to provide additional money to help someone else the next time.

That man restored my faith. It was as if he provided me an early glimpse of that day when "glorious from your heaven above shall come the city of our God." I don't know whether that man saw Jesus' face when he looked at me, but I see it in his face every time I think of him.

## PRAYER

Descend again to us, Lord Jesus! Heal the hearts of pain among the restless throngs. We need to see you. Tread the city's streets again!

*"I am already there. I have always been there. Where are you? If you can't see me, perhaps you're looking for me in the wrong place."*

Amen.

# APPENDIX

# OF NOTE

Music for many of the featured hymns are included in this appendix. While most of the tunes will be familiar to readers, in a few cases, the author selected a lesser-known tune that he felt most suitably enhanced the hymn. The lyrics may be slightly different in the sheet music than in the meditations; as the author explained in the preface, hymnal editors often revise the text of a hymn for a variety of reasons. The meaning rises above small syntactical differences. The music is included here not as a comparison of actual lyrics but as an invitation to lovers of music (and musicians) to hum, sing, or play the hymn. If a musical setting is not offered in these pages, Hymnary.org is a helpful companion.

# A MIGHTY FORTRESS IS OUR GOD

Martin Luther (1483-1546)  Tune: *Ein feste Burg*

1 A might - y for - tress is our God, a bul - wark
2 Did we in our own strength con - fide, our striv - ing
3 And though this world, with dev - ils filled, should threat - en
4 That word a - bove all earth - ly powers, no thanks to

nev - er fail - ing; our help - er he a - mid the flood
would be los - ing; were not the right man on our side,
to un - do us; we will not fear, for God hath willed
them, a - bid - eth; the Spi - rit and the gifts are ours

of mor - tal ills pre - vail - ing: for still our an - cient foe
the man of God's own choos - ing: dost ask who that may be?
his truth to tri - umph through us; the prince of dark-ness grim,
through him who with us sid - eth: let goods and kin-dred go,

doth seek to work us woe; his craft and power are great,
Christ Je - sus, it is he; Lord Sa - ba - oth his Name,
we trem - ble not for him; his rage we can en - dure,
this mor - tal life al - so; the bo - dy they may kill:

and, armed with cru - el hate, on earth is not his e - qual.
from age to age the same, and he must win the bat - tle.
for lo! his doom is sure, one lit - tle word shall fell him.
God's truth a - bid - eth still, his king - dom is for ev - er.

# ABIDE WITH ME

Henry Francis Lyte (1793-1847)

Tune: *Eventide*

1 A - bide with me: fast falls the e - ven - tide;
2 I need thy pres - ence ev - ery pass - ing hour;
3 I fear no foe, with thee at hand to bless;
4 Hold thou thy cross be - fore my clos - ing eyes;

the dark - ness deep - ens; Lord, with me a - bide:
what but thy grace can foil the tempt - er's power?
ills have no weight, and tears no bit - ter - ness.
shine through the gloom, and point me to the skies;

when o - ther help - ers fail and com - forts flee,
Who, like thy - self, my guide and stay can be?
Where is death's sting? Where, grave, thy vic - to - ry?
heaven's morn - ing breaks, and earth's vain sha - dows flee;

help of the help - less, O a - bide with me.
Through cloud and sun - shine, Lord, a - bide with me.
I tri - umph still, if thou a - bide with me.
in life, in death, O Lord, a - bide with me.

# AH, HOLY JESUS

Johann Heermann (1585-1647)  Tune: *Herzliebster Jesu*

1 Ah, ho-ly Je-sus, how hast thou of-fend-ed, that man to
2 Who was the guilt-y? Who brought this up-on thee? A-las, my
3 Lo, the Good Shep-herd for the sheep is of-fered; the slave hath
4 For me, kind Je-sus, was thy in-car-na-tion, thy mor-tal
5 There-fore, kind Je-sus, since I can-not pay thee, I do a-

1 judge thee hath in hate pre-tend-ed? By foes de-rid-ed,
2 trea-son, Je-sus, hath un-done thee. 'Twas I, Lord Je-sus,
3 sin-ned, and the Son hath suf-fered; for our a-tone-ment,
4 sor-row, and thy life's ob-la-tion; thy death of an-guish
5 dore thee, and will ev-er pray thee, think on thy pi-ty

1 by thine own re-ject-ed, O most af-flict-ed.
2 I it was de-nied thee: I cru-ci-fied thee.
3 while we noth-ing heed-ed, God in-ter-ced-ed.
4 and thy bit-ter pas-sion, for my sal-va-tion.
5 and thy love un-swerv-ing, not my de-serv-ing.

# ALLELUIA! SING TO JESUS!

William Chatterton Dix (1837-1898)  Tune: *Hyfrydol*

1 Alleluia! sing to Jesus! his the scepter, his the throne; Alleluia! his the triumph, his the victory alone; Hark! the

*2 Alleluia! not as orphans are we left in sorrow now; Alleluia! he is near us, faith believes, nor questions how: though the

3 Alleluia! bread of Heaven, Thou on earth our food, our stay! Alleluia! here the sinful flee to thee from day to day: Inter-

4 Alleluia! King eternal, thee the Lord of lords we own: Alleluia! born of Mary, earth thy footstool, heaven thy throne: thou with-

*5 Alleluia! sing to Jesus! his the scepter, his the throne; Alleluia! his the triumph, his the victory alone; Hark! the

1 songs of peace - ful Zi - on thun - der like a
2 cloud from sight re - ceived him, when the for - ty
3 ces - sor, friend of sin - ners, earth's Re - deem - er,
4 in the veil hast en - tered, robed in flesh, our
5 songs of ho - ly Zi - on thun - der like a

1 might - y flood; Je - sus out of ev - ery
2 days were o'er, shall our hearts for - get his
3 plead for me, where the songs of all the
4 great High Priest: thou on earth both Priest and
5 might - y flood; Je - sus out of ev - ery

1 na - tion hath re - deemed us by his blood.
2 prom - ise, "I am with you ev - er - more"?
3 sin - less sweep a - cross the crys - tal sea.
4 Vic - tim in the eu - cha - ris - tic feast.
5 na - tion hath re - deemed us by his blood.

# AMAZING GRACE

John Newton (1725-1807)

Tune: *New Britain*

*The melody may be sung in canon at distances of either two or three beats.*

# COME, LABOR ON

Jane Laurie Borthwick (1813-1897)                    Tune: *Ora Labora*

1 Come, la - bor on. Who dares stand i - dle
2 Come, la - bor on. The en - e - my is
3 Come, la - bor on. A - way with gloom - y
4 Come, la - bor on. Claim the high call - ing
5 Come, la - bor on. No time for rest, till

1 on the har - vest plain, while all a - round us
2 watch - ing night and day, to sow the tares, to
3 doubts and faith - less fear! No arm so weak but
4 an - gels can - not share— to young and old the
5 glows the west - ern sky, till the long sha - dows

1 waves the gold - en grain? And to each ser - vant
2 snatch the seed a - way; while we in sleep our
3 may do ser - vice here: by feeb - lest a - gents
4 Gos - pel glad - ness bear: re - deem the time; its
5 o'er our path - way lie, and a glad sound comes

1 does the Mas - ter say, "Go work to - day."
2 du - ty have for - got, he slum - bered___ not.
3 may our God ful - fill his right - eous___ will.
4 hours too swift - ly fly. The night draws___ nigh.
5 with the set - ting sun,___ "Ser - vants, well done."

# COME, THOU FOUNT OF EVERY BLESSING

Robert Robinson (1735-1790)

Tune: *Nettleton*

1 Come, thou fount of ev-ery bless-ing, tune my
2 Here I find my great-est trea-sure; hith-er,
3 Oh, to grace how great a debt-or dai-ly

heart to sing thy grace! Streams of mer-cy nev-er
by thy help, I've come; and I hope, by thy good
I'm con-strained to be! Let thy good-ness, like a

ceas-ing, call for songs of loud-est praise.
plea-sure, safe-ly to ar-rive at home.
fet-ter, bind my wan-dering heart to thee:

Teach me some me-lo-dious son - net, sung by
Je-sus sought me when a stran - ger wan-dering
prone to wan-der, Lord, I feel it, prone to

flam-ing tongues a-bove. Praise the mount! Oh, fix me
from the fold of God; he, to res-cue me from
leave the God I love; here's my heart, oh, take and

on it, mount of God's un-chang-ing love.
dan-ger, in-ter-posed his pre-cious blood.
seal it, seal it for thy courts a-bove.

# FAIREST LORD JESUS

Anonymous, 17<sup>th</sup> century

Tune: *St. Elizabeth*

1 Fair - est Lord Je - sus, Ru-ler of all na - ture, O thou of
2 Fair are the mea - dows, fair-er still the wood - lands, robed in the
3 Fair is the sun - shine, fair-er still the moon - light, and all the

God and man the Son; thee will I cher - ish,
bloom - ing garb of spring: Je - sus is fair - er,
twink - ling, star - ry host: Je - sus shines bright - er,

thee will I hon - or, thou, my soul's glo - ry, joy, and crown.
Je - sus is pur - er, who makes the woe-ful heart to sing.
Je - sus shines pur - er, than all the an-gels heaven can boast.

# GOD OF GRACE AND GOD OF GLORY

Harry E. Fosdick (1878-1969)

Tune: *Cwm Rhondda*

1 God of grace and God of glo - ry, on thy peo - ple pour thy power;
2 Lo! the hosts of e - vil round us scorn thy Christ, as - sail his ways!
3 Cure thy chil - dren's war - ring mad - ness, bend our pride to thy con - trol;
4 Save us from weak res - ig - na - tion to the e - vils we de - plore;

crown thine an - cient Church's sto - ry; bring her bud to glo - rious flower.
From the fears that long have bound us free our hearts to faith and praise:
shame our wan - ton, self - ish glad - ness, rich in things and poor in soul.
let the gift of thy sal - va - tion be our glo - ry ev - er - more.

Grant us wis - dom, grant us cour - age, for the fac - ing of this
grant us wis - dom, grant us cour - age for the liv - ing of these
Grant us wis - dom, grant us cour - age, lest we miss thy king - dom's
Grant us wis - dom, grant us cour - age, serv - ing thee whom we a -

hour, for the fac - ing of this hour.
days, for the liv - ing of these days.
goal, lest we miss thy king - dom's goal.
dore, serv - ing thee whom we a - dore.

# GUIDE ME, O THOU GREAT JEHOVAH

William Williams (1717-1791)

Tune: *Cwm Rhondda*

1 Guide me, O thou great Je - ho - vah, pil - grim through this
2 O - pen now the crys - tal foun-tain, whence the heal - ing
3 When I tread the verge of Jor - dan, bid my anx - ious

bar - ren land; I am weak, but thou art might - y;
stream doth flow; let the fire and cloud - y pil - lar
fears sub - side; death of death, and hell's de - struc - tion,

hold me with thy power - ful hand; bread of hea - ven,
lead me all my jour - ney through; strong de - liv - erer,
land me safe on Ca - naan's side; songs of prais - es,

bread of hea - ven, feed me now and ev - er -
strong de - liv - erer, be thou still my strength and
songs of prais - es, I will ev - er give to

more, feed me now and ev - er - more.
shield, be thou still my strength and shield.
thee, I will ev - er give to thee.

# HILLS OF THE NORTH, REJOICE

Charles Edward Oakley (1802-1880)　　　　　　　　Tune: *Little Cornard*

Hills of the North, rejoice;
River and mountain spring,
Hark to the advent voice;
Valley and lowland, sing;
Though absent long, your Lord is nigh;
He judgment brings and victory.

Isles of the southern seas,
Deep in your coral caves
Pent be each warring breeze,
Lulled be your restless waves:
He comes to reign with boundless sway,
And makes your wastes His great highway.

Lands of the East, awake,
Soon shall your sons be free;
The sleep of ages break,
And rise to liberty.
On your far hills, long cold and gray,
Has dawned the everlasting day.

Shores of the utmost West,
Ye that have waited long,
Unvisited, unblest,
Break forth to swelling song;
High raise the note, that Jesus died,
Yet lives and reigns, the Crucified.

Shout, while ye journey home;
Songs be in every mouth;
Lo, from the North we come,
From East, and West, and South.
City of God, the bond are free,
We come to live and reign in thee!

# HOW FIRM A FOUNDATION

Anonymous, 18<sup>th</sup> century

Tune: *Foundation*

1 How firm a foun - da - tion, ye saints of the Lord,
2 "Fear not, I am with thee; O be not dis - mayed!
3 "When through the deep wa - ters I call thee to go,
4 "When through fier - y tri - als thy path - way shall lie,
5 "The soul that to Je - sus hath fled for re - pose,

1 is laid for your faith in his ex - cel - lent word!
2 For I am thy God, and will still give thee aid;
3 the riv - ers of woe shall not thee o - ver - flow;
4 my grace, all - suf - fi - cient, shall be thy sup - ply;
5 I will not, I will not de - sert to its foes;

1 What more can he say than to you he hath said,
2 I'll strength - en thee, help thee, and cause thee to stand,
3 for I will be with thee, thy trou - bles to bless,
4 the flame shall not hurt thee; I on - ly de - sign
5 that soul, though all hell shall en - deav - or to shake,

1 to you that for ref - uge to Je - sus have fled?
2 up - held by my right - eous, om - ni - po - tent hand.
3 and sanc - ti - fy to thee thy deep - est dis - tress.
4 thy dross to con - sume, and thy gold to re - fine.
5 I'll nev - er, no, nev - er, no, nev - er for - sake."

Optional Interlude

# IMMORTAL, INVISIBLE, GOD ONLY WISE

Walter C. Smith (1824-1908)                                    Tune: *St. Denio*

1 Im - mor - tal, in - vis - i - ble, God on - ly wise,
2 Un - rest - ing, un - hast - ing, and si - lent as light,
3 To all life thou giv - est, to both great and small;
4 Thou reign - est in glo - ry, thou rul - est in light,

in light in - ac - ces - si - ble hid from our eyes,
nor want - ing, nor wast - ing, thou rul - est in might;
in all life thou liv - est, the true life of all;
thine an - gels a - dore thee, all veil - ing their sight;

most bless - ed, most glo - rious, the An - cient of Days,
thy jus - tice like moun - tains high soar - ing a - bove
we blos - som and flour - ish, like leaves on the tree,
all laud we would ren - der: O help us to see

al - might - y, vic - tor - ious, thy great Name we praise.
thy clouds, which are foun - tains of good - ness and love.
then with - er and per - ish; but nought chan - geth thee.
'tis on - ly the splen - dor of light hid - eth thee.

# IT CAME UPON A MIDNIGHT CLEAR

Edmund H. Sears (1810-1876)                    Tune: *Carol*

1 It came up - on the mid - night clear, that
2 Still through the clov - en skies they come with
3 Yet with the woes of sin and strife the
4 For lo! the days are haste - ning on, by

glo - rious song of old, from an - gels bend - ing
peace - ful wings un - furled, and still their heaven - ly
world has suf - fered long; be - neath the heaven - ly
pro - phets seen of old, when with the ev - er -

near the earth to touch their harps of gold:
mu - sic floats o'er all the wea - ry world;
hymn have rolled two thou - sand years of wrong;
cir - cling years shall come the time fore - told,

"Peace on the earth, good will to men, from
a - bove its sad and low - ly plains they
and war - ring hu - man - kind hears not the
when peace shall o - ver all the earth its

heaven's all - gra - cious King." The world in sol - emn
bend on hov - ering wing, and ev - er o'er its
tid - ings which they bring; O hush the noise and
an - cient splen - dors fling, and all the world give

still - ness lay to hear the an - gels sing.
Ba - bel - sounds the bless - ed an - gels sing.
cease your strife and hear the an - gels sing!
back the song which now the an - gels sing.

# JESUS, LOVER OF MY SOUL

Charles Wesley (1707-1788)                                  Tune: *Aberystwyth*

1 Je - sus, Lov - er of my soul, let me to thy bos - om
2 O - ther ref - uge have I none, hangs my help - less soul on
3 Plen-teous grace with thee is found, grace to cleanse from ev - ery

fly, while the near - er wa - ters roll, while the tem-pest
thee; leave, ah! leave me not a - lone, still sup - port and
sin; let the heal - ing streams a - bound, make and keep me

still is high: hide me, O my Sa - vior, hide,
com - fort me! All my trust on thee is stayed;
pure with - in. Thou of life the foun - tain art,

till the storm of life be past; safe in - to the
all my help from thee I bring; cov - er my de -
free - ly let me take of thee: spring thou up with -

ha - ven guide, O re - ceive my soul at last.
fense - less head with the sha - dow of thy wing.
in my heart, rise to all e - ter - ni - ty.

# LEAD, KINDLY LIGHT

John Henry Newman (1801-1890)

Tune: *Lux Benigna*

1. Lead, kind-ly Light, a-mid th'en-cir-cling gloom, Lead Thou me on;
2. I was not ev-er thus, nor prayed that Thou Shouldst lead me on;
3. So long Thy power hath blest me, sure it still Will lead me on,

The night is dark, and I am far from home; Lead Thou me on:
I loved to choose and see my path; but now Lead Thou me on.
O'er moor and fen, o'er crag and tor-rent, till The night is gone;

Keep Thou my feet; I do not ask to see
I loved the gar-ish day, and, spite of fears,
And with the morn those an-gel fa-ces smile,

The dis-tant scene— one step e-nough for me.
Pride ruled my will: re-mem-ber not past years.
Which I have loved long since, and lost a-while. A-MEN.

# LIFT EVERY VOICE AND SING

James Weldon Johnson (1871-1938)                    Tune: *Lift Every Voice*

1 Lift ev-ery voice and sing till earth and hea - ven ring, ring with the
2 Ston - y the road we trod, bit - ter the chas-tening rod, felt in the
3 God of our wea - ry years, God of our si - lent tears, thou who hast

har - mon - ies of lib - er - ty. Let our re-joic-ing rise
days when hope un - born had died; yet, with a stead-y beat,
brought us thus far on the way; thou who hast by thy might

high as the lis - tening skies; let it re - sound loud as the
have not our wea - ry feet come to the place for which our
led us in - to the light; keep us for ev - er in the

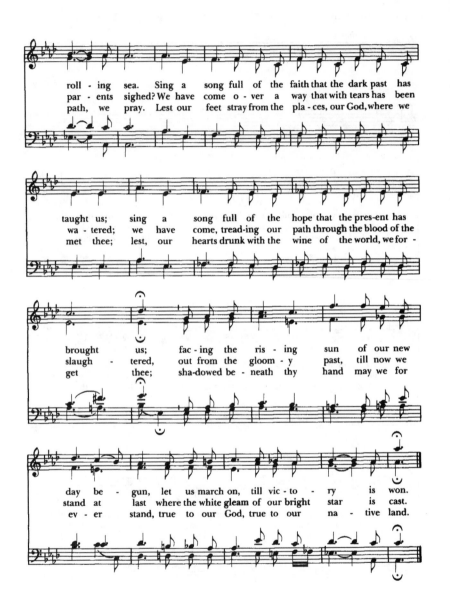

roll - ing sea. Sing a song full of the faith that the dark past has
par - ents sighed? We have come o - ver a way that with tears has been
path, we pray. Lest our feet stray from the pla - ces, our God, where we

taught us; sing a song full of the hope that the pres-ent has
wa - tered; we have come, tread-ing our path through the blood of the
met thee; lest, our hearts drunk with the wine of the world, we for -

brought us; fac-ing the ris - ing sun of our new
slaugh - tered, out from the gloom - y past, till now we
get thee; sha-dowed be - neath thy hand may we for

day be - gun, let us march on, till vic-to - ry is won.
stand at last where the white gleam of our bright star is cast.
ev - er stand, true to our God, true to our na - tive land.

# LO! HE COMES WITH CLOUDS DESCENDING

Charles Wesley (1707-1788)

Tune: *Helmsley*

1  Lo! he comes, with clouds de - scend - ing, once for our sal - va - tion slain; thou - sand thou - sand saints at - tend - ing swell the tri - umph of his train: Al - le - lu - ia! Al - le - lu - ia! Al - le - lu - ia! Christ the Lord re - turns to reign.

2  Ev - ery eye shall now be - hold him, robed in dread - ful ma - jes - ty; those who set at nought and sold him, pierced, and nailed him to the tree, deep - ly wail - ing, deep - ly wail - ing, deep - ly wail - ing, shall the true Mes - si - ah see.

3  Those dear tok - ens of his pas - sion still his daz - zling bo - dy bears, cause of end - less ex - ul - ta - tion to his ran - somed wor - ship - ers; with what rap - ture, with what rap - ture, with what rap - ture gaze we on those glo - rious scars!

4  Yea, a - men! let all a - dore thee, high on thine e - ter - nal throne; Sa - vior, take the power and glo - ry; claim the king - dom for thine own: Al - le - lu - ia! Al - le - lu - ia! Al - le - lu - ia! Thou shalt reign, and thou a - lone.

# MAKE ME A CAPTIVE, LORD

Rev. George Matheson (1842-1906)                    Tune: *Llanllyfni*

*Moderately slow*

1. Make me a cap-tive, Lord, And then I shall be free;
2. My heart is weak and poor Un-til it mas-ter find;
3. My power is faint and low Till I have learned to serve;
4. My will is not my own Till Thou hast made it Thine;

Force me to ren-der up my sword, And I shall con-queror be.
It has no spring of ac-tion sure— It va-ries with the wind.
It wants the need-ed fire to glow, It wants the breeze to nerve;
If it would reach a mon-arch's throne It must its crown re-sign;

I sink in life's a-larms When by my-self I stand;
It can-not free-ly move Till Thou hast wrought its chain;
It can-not drive the world Un-til it-self be driven;
It on-ly stands un-bent A-mid the clash-ing strife,

Im-pris-on me with-in Thine arms, And strong shall be my hand.
En-slave it with Thy match-less love, And death-less it shall reign.
Its flag can on-ly be un-furled When Thou shalt breathe from heaven.
When on Thy bos-om it has leant And found in Thee its life. A-MEN.

# O FOR A THOUSAND TONGUES TO SING

Charles Wesley (1707-1788)                                   Tune: *Azmon*

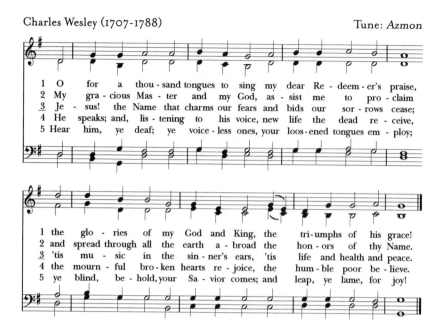

1 O for a thou-sand tongues to sing my dear Re-deem-er's praise,
2 My gra-cious Mas-ter and my God, as-sist me to pro-claim
3 Je-sus! the Name that charms our fears and bids our sor-rows cease;
4 He speaks; and, lis-tening to his voice, new life the dead re-ceive,
5 Hear him, ye deaf; ye voice-less ones, your loos-ened tongues em-ploy;

1 the glo-ries of my God and King, the tri-umphs of his grace!
2 and spread through all the earth a-broad the hon-ors of thy Name.
3 'tis mu-sic in the sin-ner's ears, 'tis life and health and peace.
4 the mourn-ful bro-ken hearts re-joice, the hum-ble poor be-lieve.
5 ye blind, be-hold, your Sa-vior comes; and leap, ye lame, for joy!

6 Glory to God and praise and love
    be now and ever given
  by saints below and saints above,
    the Church in earth and heaven.

# O JESUS, I HAVE PROMISED

John Ernest Bode (1816-1874)                                    Tune: *Nyland*

1 O Je - sus, I have prom-ised to serve thee to the end:
2 O let me hear thee speak-ing in ac - cents clear and still,
3 O Je - sus, thou hast prom-ised to all who fol - low thee,

be thou for ev - er near me, my Mas - ter and my friend;
a - bove the storms of pas-sion, the mur-murs of self - will;
that where thou art in glo - ry there shall thy ser - vant be;

I shall not fear the bat - tle, if thou art by my side,
O speak to re - as - sure me, to has - ten or con - trol;
and, Je - sus, I have prom - ised to serve thee to the end;

nor wan - der from the path - way, if thou wilt be my guide.
O speak, and make me lis - ten, thou guard-ian of my soul.
O give me grace to fol - low, my Mas - ter and my friend.

# O LITTLE TOWN OF BETHLEHEM

Phillips Brooks (1835-1893)                    Tune: *St. Louis*

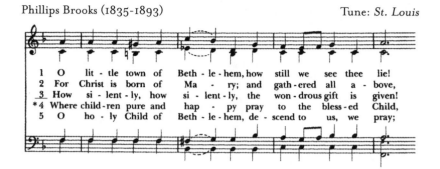

1 O lit - tle town of Beth - le - hem, how still we see thee lie!
2 For Christ is born of Ma - ry; and gath - ered all a - bove,
3 How si - lent - ly, how si - lent - ly, the won - drous gift is given!
*4 Where child - ren pure and hap - py pray to the bless - ed Child,
5 O ho - ly Child of Beth - le - hem, de - scend to us, we pray;

1 A - bove thy deep and dream - less sleep the si - lent stars go by;
2 while mor - tals sleep, the an - gels keep their watch of won - dering love.
3 So God im - parts to hu - man hearts the bless - ings of his heaven.
4 where mis - er - y cries out to thee, Son of the mo - ther mild;
5 cast out our sin and en - ter in, be born in us to - day.

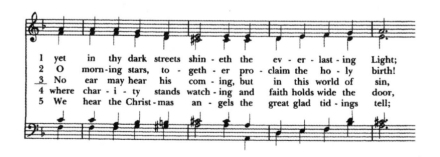

1 yet in thy dark streets shin - eth the ev - er - last - ing Light;
2 O morn - ing stars, to - geth - er pro - claim the ho - ly birth!
3 No ear may hear his com - ing, but in this world of sin,
4 where char - i - ty stands watch - ing and faith holds wide the door,
5 We hear the Christ - mas an - gels the great glad tid - ings tell;

# O LOVE, HOW DEEP, HOW BROAD, HOW HIGH

tr. Benjamin Webb (1819-1885)                    Tune: *Deus tourum militum*

1 O love, how deep, how broad, how high, how pass - ing
2 For us bap - tized, for us he bore his ho - ly
3 For us he prayed; for us he taught; for us his
4 For us to wick - ed hands be - trayed, scourged, mocked, in
5 For us he rose from death a - gain; for us he
6 All glo - ry to our Lord and God for love so

1 thought and fan - ta - sy, that God, the Son of
2 fast and hun - gered sore; for us temp - ta - tions
3 dai - ly works he wrought: by words and signs and
4 pur - ple robe ar - rayed, he bore the shame - ful
5 went on high to reign; for us he sent his
6 deep, so high, so broad; the Trin - i - ty whom

1 God, should take our mor - tal form for mor - tals' sake.
2 sharp he knew; for us the tempt - er ov - er - threw.
3 ac - tions, thus still seek - ing not him - self, but us.
4 cross and death; for us gave up his dy - ing breath.
5 Spi - rit here to guide, to strength - en, and to cheer.
6 we a - dore for ev - er and for ev - er - more.

# O LOVE THAT WILT NOT LET ME GO

George Matheson (1842-1906)

Tune: *St. Margaret*

1 O Love that will not let me go,
I rest my weary soul in thee;
I give thee back the life I owe,
that in thine ocean depths its flow may richer, fuller be.

2 O Light that fol - lowest all my way,
I yield my flick - ering torch to thee;
my heart re - stores its bor - rowed ray,
that in thy sun - shine's blaze its day may brigh - ter, fair - er be.

3 O Joy that seek - est me through pain,
I can - not close my heart to thee;
I trace the rain - bow through the rain,
that morn shall tear - less be.

4 O Cross that lift - est up my head,
I dare not ask to fly from thee;
I lay in dust life's glo - ry dead,
from the ground there blos - soms red life that shall end - less be.

# ONCE TO EVERY MAN AND NATION

James Russell Lowell (1845)

Tune: *Ebenezer*

1. Once to ev - ery man and na - tion, Comes the mo - ment to de - cide,
2. Then to side with truth is no - ble, When we share her wretch - ed crust,
3. By the light of burn - ing mar - tyrs, Christ, Thy bleed - ing feet we track,
4. Though the cause of e - vil pros - per, Yet the truth a - lone is strong;

In the strife of truth with false - hood, For the good or e - vil side;
Ere her cause bring fame and pro - fit, And 'tis pros - perous to be just;
Toil - ing up new Cal - v'ries ev - er, With the cross that turns not back;
Though her por - tion be the scaf - fold, And up - on the throne be wrong;

Some great cause, some great de - ci - sion, Off - ering each the bloom or blight,
Then it is the brave man choos - es While the cow - ard stands a - side,
New oc - ca - sions teach new du - ties, Time makes an - cient good un - couth,
Yet that scaf - fold sways the fu - ture, And be - hind the dim un - known,

And the choice goes by for - ev - er, 'Twixt that dark - ness and that light.
Till the mul - ti - tude make vir - tue Of the faith they had de - nied.
They must up - ward still and on - ward, Who would keep a - breast of truth.
Stand - eth God with - in the sha - dow, Keep - ing watch a - bove His own.

# ONWARD, CHRISTIAN SOLDIERS

Sabine Baring-Gould (1834-1924)                    Tune: *St. Gertrude*

1  On - ward, Chris - tian sol - diers, march - ing as to war,
*2  At the sign of tri - umph Sa - tan's host doth flee;
*3  Like a might - y ar - my moves the Church of God;
4  Crowns and thrones may per - ish, king - doms rise and wane,
5  On - ward, then, ye peo - ple, join our hap - py throng;

1  with the cross of Je - sus go - ing on be - fore!
2  on, then, Chris - tian sol - diers, on to vic - to - ry!
3  Chris - tians, we are tread - ing where the saints have trod;
4  but the Church of Je - sus con - stant will re - main;
5  blend with ours your voic - es in the tri - umph song:

1  Christ, the roy - al Mas - ter, leads a - gainst the foe;
2  Hell's foun - da - tions quiv - er at the shout of praise;
3  we are not di - vid - ed, all one bo - dy we,
4  gates of hell can nev - er 'gainst that Church pre - vail;
5  glo - ry, laud, and hon - or, un - to Christ the King;

1 for - ward  in - to  bat - tle,  see, his ban - ners  go.
2 Chris - tians,  lift  your  voic - es,  loud your an - thems  raise.
3 one  in  hope  and  doc - trine,  one  in  char - i - ty.
4 we  have  Christ's own  prom - ise,  and that can - not  fail.
5 this  through  count - less  a - ges  we with an - gels  sing.

*Refrain*

On - ward, Chris - tian  sol - diers,  march - ing  as  to  war,

with  the  cross  of  Je - sus  go - ing  on  be - fore!

# PRAISE, MY SOUL, THE KING OF HEAVEN

Henry F. Lyte (1793-1847)

Tune: *Lauda anima*

1 Praise, my soul, the King of heav - en; to his feet your trib - ute bring. Ran - somed, healed, re - stored, for - gi - ven, ev - er - more his prais - es sing. Al - le - lu - ia, al - le - lu - ia! Praise the ev - er - last - ing King!

The accompaniment for stanza 2 may be used for all stanzas.

3 Fa - ther - like he tends and spares us; well our fee - ble frame he knows. In his hand he gent - ly bears us, res - cues us from all our foes. Al - le - lu - ia, al - le - lu - ia! Wide - ly yet his mer - cy flows!

4 Angels, help us to adore him; you behold him face to face. Sun and moon, bow down before him, dwellers all in time and space. Alleluia, alleluia! Praise with us the God of grace!

# THE CHURCH'S ONE FOUNDATION

Samuel J. Stone (1839-1900)

Tune: *Aurelia*

1 The Church's one foun - da - tion is Je - sus Christ her Lord;
2 E - lect from ev - ery na - tion, yet one o'er all the earth,
3 Though with a scorn - ful won - der men see her sore op - pressed,
4 Mid toil and tri - bu - la - tion, and tu - mult of her war
5 Yet she on earth hath un - ion with God, the Three in One,

1 she is his new cre - a - tion by wa - ter and the word:
2 her char - ter of sal - va - tion, one Lord, one faith, one birth;
3 by schi - sms rent a - sun - der, by her - e - sies dis - tressed;
4 she waits the con - sum - ma - tion of peace for ev - er - more;
5 and mys - tic sweet com - mun - ion with those whose rest is won.

1 from heaven he came and sought her to be his ho - ly bride;
2 one ho - ly Name she bless - es, par - takes one ho - ly food,
3 yet saints their watch are keep - ing, their cry goes up, "How long?"
4 till with the vi - sion glo - rious her long - ing eyes are blessed,
5 O hap - py ones and ho - ly! Lord, give us grace that we

1 with his own blood he bought her, and for her life he died.
2 and to one hope she press - es, with ev - ery grace en - dued.
3 and soon the night of weep - ing shall be the morn of song.
4 and the great Church vic - to - rious shall be the Church at rest.
5 like them, the meek and low - ly, on high may dwell with thee.

# THE DAY THOU GAVEST, LORD, IS ENDED

John Ellerton (1826-1893)  Tune: *St. Clement*

1 The day thou gav - est, Lord, is end - ed, the dark - ness
2 We thank thee that thy Church, un - sleep-ing while earth rolls
3 As o'er each con - ti - nent and is - land the dawn leads
4 So be it, Lord; thy throne shall nev - er, like earth's proud

falls at thy be - hest; to thee our morn - ing hymns a -
on - ward in - to light, through all the world her watch is
on an - oth - er day, the voice of prayer is nev - er
em - pires, pass a - way; thy king - dom stands, and grows for

scend - ed, thy praise shall sanc - ti - fy our rest.
keep - ing, and rests not now by day or night.
si - lent, nor dies the strain of praise a - way.
ev - er, till all thy crea - tures own thy sway.

*This hymn may be used in the morning by omitting stanza 1.*

# WHEN I SURVEY THE WONDEROUS CROSS

Isaac Watts (1674-1748)

Tune: *Rockingham*

1 When I sur - vey the won - drous cross where the young
2 For - bid it, Lord, that I should boast, save in the
3 See, from his head, his hands, his feet sor - row and
4 Were the whole realm of na - ture mine, that were an

Prince of Glo - ry died, my rich - est gain I
cross of Christ, my God: all the vain things that
love flow min - gled down! Did e'er such love and
of - fering far too small; love so a - maz - ing,

count but loss, and pour con - tempt on all my pride.
charm me most, I sac - ri - fice them to his blood.
sor - row meet, or thorns com - pose so rich a crown?
so di - vine, de - mands my soul, my life, my all.

# WHERE CROSS THE CROWDED WAYS OF LIFE

Frank Mason North (1850-1935)

Tune: *Gardiner*

1 Where cross the crowd-ed ways of life, where sound the
2 In haunts of wretch-ed - ness and need, on sha-dowed
3 The cup of wa - ter given for thee still holds the
4 O Mas - ter, from the moun - tain side, make haste to
5 till all the world shall learn thy love, and fol - low

1 cries of race and clan, a - bove the noise of
2 thresh-olds dark with fears, from paths where hide the
3 fresh - ness of thy grace; yet long these mul - ti -
4 heal these hearts of pain; a - mong these rest - less
5 where thy feet have trod; till glo - rious from thy

1 self - ish strife, we hear thy voice, O Son of Man.
2 lures of greed, we catch the vi - sion of thy tears.
3 tudes to see the true com - pas - sion of thy face.
4 throngs a - bide, O tread the ci - ty's streets a - gain;
5 heaven a - bove, shall come the ci - ty of our God.

# ACKNOWLEDGMENTS

I am grateful to several friends and colleagues who read this or an earlier draft of these meditations and offered helpful suggestions for organizing them and improving the clarity of my prose. They are Richelle Thompson, my editor at Forward Movement in Cincinnati, Ohio; Janet Buening, also of Cincinnati; the Rev. Albert and Nancy Kennington of Fairhope, Alabama; the Rev. John and Ann Phillips of Pensacola, Florida; Betsy Rogers of Belleville, Illinois; Eileen Head of Fairhope, Alabama; Marilyn Owens of Fairhope, Alabama; Tim and Cindy Op'tHolt of Daphne, Alabama; Mike Gilbert, an inmate at the James Crabtree Correctional Center in Helena, Oklahoma; and my wife, Pamela H. Schmidt. Thanks to each of you for the gift of your time and wisdom.

# ABOUT THE AUTHOR

Richard H. Schmidt, a native of Shelbyville, Kentucky, was editor and director of Forward Movement from 2005 until his retirement in 2011. He has served Episcopal congregations in four dioceses in the United States and has taught in England and Nigeria. This is his seventh book. Schmidt lives with his wife of fifty years, Pamela, in Fairhope, Alabama.

# ABOUT FORWARD MOVEMENT

Forward Movement inspires disciples and empowers evangelists. Our mission is to support you in your spiritual journey, to help you grow as a follower of Jesus Christ. We live out our ministry by publishing books, daily reflections, studies for small groups, and online resources. *Forward Day by Day* is read daily by Christians around the world and is also available in Spanish (*Adelenta Día a Día*) and Braille, online, as a podcast, and as an app for your smartphones or tablets. We donate nearly 30,000 copies each quarter to prisons, hospitals, and nursing homes. We actively seek partners across the church and look for ways to provide resources that inspire and challenge.

A ministry of the Episcopal Church for more than eighty years, Forward Movement is a nonprofit organization funded by sales of resources and gifts from generous donors.

To learn more about Forward Movement and its resources, please visit www.ForwardMovement.org. We are delighted to be doing this work and invite your prayers and support.